Carlyle Marney

PRIESTS TO EACH OTHER

Judson Press,® Valley Forge

PRIESTS TO EACH OTHER

Library of Congress Cataloging in Publication Data

Marney, Carlyle, 1916-
    Priests to each other.

    Includes bibliographical references.
    1. Laity. 2. Priesthood, Universal. I. Title.
BV4525.M37   262'.15   73-16787
ISBN 0-8170-0628-1

TABLE OF CONTENTS

for

Joe Carrington, James Peal
Boyd Moody, Zollie Steakley

priests of mine

INTRODUCTION

THE ONLY PRIEST
A hearer with any other

As has happened before, the last paragraphs of something done, reaching in the dark, brought out into the half-light furnish the point of departure for a new stretch of the road.

Following new half-light can be both expensive and painful. It can and does issue in a falling off into dark nights for weeks on end. It can make one see the day of his ordination as the worst of his days of infamy; it can make him curse his youthy gullibility and damn the managed credulity into which he bought, except that it's all so far behind and cannot really be retracted; so most days he lets it go.

But why did I leave that high mahogany pulpit? Why did I give up the joys and grace of the weekly proclamation? Why did I turn away from the hearing-telling-being-heard of a pastorate that brought me little but the deepest kind of satisfaction? What did I lay my hand on in that last chapter of *The Coming Faith*[1] that has put me here on the north side of Wolf Pen mountain reaching for insights I have not got?

Whatever, it's something about the gospel and the mess we have made of its genius to call man from his distortions of manhood in Creation. When we separated power from love and justice and opted for power, we came up with a fatal-to-the-gospel series of substitutes:

clergy for laity, rank for brotherhood, learning for devotement, function over relation, prestige for integrity, institution for fellowship, committees instead of service, property for community, and ritual in place of liturgy. In short, we turned from communion, work-service, and the free dance around a proper altar which is worship *(koinonia, diakonia,* and *leiturgia)*—all in the name of organized service to God.

What if a kept clergy is always a harlotry? What if, as Krister Stendahl put it at a party, "no prophet has a salary"? What if clergy have a fatal disadvantage and have largely missed the meaning of their role? What if usurpation of place and power on a grand scale has emptied the only priesthood of its power to bless? And what if clergy cannot give this power of the priesthood back, even symbolically by defrocking themselves, but laymen have to come and take it?

"*These* laymen I see," you say. Not yet and not hardly! They have been abused, misused, and confused. They've been brought into what Stewart Newman calls an "attendance button empire" ruled by "a hierarchy which is the epitome of success through the system." What if "the more mature and able a man is the more broken he may become, given the job-situation in which he is trying to achieve his ministry" among a laity almost wholly (and with large justification) anticlerical?[2] What if the whole house is sick, so sick that the gospel must evacuate on the backs of those who have been denied their heritage as priests, the only priests? Just what if our tamed lay house cats should find out that they really are "Christ, the Tiger," and that we defanged them by turning away from Luther's terrible (Vocation) *Beruf* and de-clawed them by refusing his threatening Priesthood of the Believer? "By dignifying man's calling in life as being of God, secular life was once more placed on an equal plane with the Christian ministry."[3] Luther's first reference to the principle of Priesthood of the Believer apparently came on Christmas Day, 1520, in his *Long Sermon on Usury.*[4] With his *Address to the German Nobility, The Babylonian Captivity of the Church,* and *The Freedom of the Christian,* Luther forged an entirely new concept of the obligation of laymen as priests. They were to correct abuses even of preaching and the sacraments as well as in secular life! The influence of the *Address* on German nobility was incalculable. By all three tracts plus dozens of passages in *Sermons* and *Expositions of Scripture,* etc., peasants were led to believe that the priesthood of the believer applied especially to them. It is said that peasants were able to discuss Erasmus's, Murner's, and Luther's works, while the concept of universal priesthood became dynamite potentially in the hands of the unrestrained masses.

We Christians have been given a mighty weapon—the conviction that the Man Christ can make us whole, and that men who are being made whole can create a well society aiming to keep the world out and to bring the world in. The Christian church has been a failure at both. We have neither kept the worldliness out nor have we brought the world in. Relevant Christianity requires the healing of the inhabited world of men, and this demands a new priesthood: a priesthood that believes in the redemption of the world, not the redemption of the church. For centuries the church has refused to see the need to put a priest at every elbow. No professional clergy can do what the church is called to do.

I

It is morally certain that some change is on the way, something like the changes that occurred during the Luther-Calvin-Zwingli-Wesley times. The church in its present forms cannot get through. We are blocked, and we choke. The forms we have loved will be shattered. This insight is not pessimistic; it is practical and hopeful, and it rests on the realization that this has happened before. I am morally certain that, as before, the seed of the New Reformation was in the old one and that this seed is now in the form of a still unexploited insight of the great Martin Luther. The "priest at every elbow" means that we are "priests to each other," the "priesthood of every believer." But we have perverted this. Since 1640, on this continent we have elevated the clergy into a kept harlotry. This coronation didn't go too well. We have proliferated the "calling" until now it is broken into little specialties. We have multiplied institutions and orders and organizations masking the needs behind the robe, the title, and the office; we have increased function and form over relation and redemption, and we do this in order to evade the cat on our own back which is our own priesthood. The result has been the creation of a schizophrenic ministry that does not know what it is for, and a confused laity being used for the wrong ends.

Graydon McClellan, in *New Frontiers of Christianity* characterizes the modern laymen's movement. He says it

> evidences an unease in the churches, but [it] represents no real surge of power. It points up the inevitable restiveness of Protestant laymen whose birthright ministry is carried on by ordained deputies, but it will dead-end in frustration because it is an unconscious rebellion against the clergy rather than the flower of a new partnership between pastors and a people.[5]

The lay movement is really an *anti-preacher* movement! This movement is stronger than ever now and it is justified. We clergy think too much in terms of "keeping laymen busy," when we ourselves deplore the "busy work of the pastorate." We talk in terms of "using more laymen" when we ourselves despise "being used." We talk about "holding up the hands of the pastor" when we ourselves care very little about the role of assisting somebody else's pastorate. All this is designed to elevate the pastor and to "bring in the sheaves." Now I'm all for bringing in the sheaves if the bringing in makes any difference. We used to sing another song every Sunday: "Bring Them In." But not many ever did come in "from the fields of sin."

In spite of the fifty-year loyalty to thousands of churches begun in Baracca movements, men's classes, and Billy Sunday lay groups, we simply never did get to the forces of *labor* or of *commerce*. No church ever has. We never did really bring them in. We never will. It cannot happen if it waits on us to get them *here,* where the church is a successful blesser of a successful culture and pastors are hired to make it go!

This, all this, is the most incredible perversion of the believer's competent priesthood in Christendom! And the result—the result? Said Luther, ". . . they who think they now are gourmandizing the gospel have not yet even begun to eat."[6] To the Elector Frederick he wrote, ". . . if the condition that exists in Wittenberg existed in Leipzig, I would go to Leipzig even if . . . it rained Duke Georges for nine days and every duke were nine times as furious as this one. *He takes my Lord Christ to be a man of straw!"*[7]

Now we are serious here, and we want the gospel. What shall we do? We must recover the priesthood of every believer or we can't *do* at all. We must discover that we really are "priests to each other," for every man needs a priest at his elbow.

II

In the spring of 1507 Martin Luther became a priest, celebrated his first Mass, and was so awed by the mystery of it all, along with the weight of his own guilt and identity crisis, that he had some kind of fit in the choir and fell over crying, "It's not me; it's not me," to his acute embarrassment.[8] His father had come, with twenty horses to his carriages, carrying a gift of twenty golden gulden, to see his son made a priest of the church. In less than twenty years Martin Luther was writing of the professional priesthood, "Behold the noble, precious priesthood! . . . Has there ever been such a foolish, childish, and senseless priesthood even among the heathen? . . . O dear Lord Jesus. . . . !"[9]

In the letter "To the Illustrious Senate and People of Prague," he said, ". . . one who has earned the noose or the wheel among the Germans qualifies as priest among the Bohemians."[10] And things being as they were in Prague,

> I would confidently advise that you have no ministers at all. For it would be safer and more wholesome for the father of the house to read the gospel and . . . to baptize those who are born in his home, and so to govern himself and his according to the doctrine of Christ, even if throughout life they did not dare or could not receive the [Lord's Supper]. . . .

If in this way two, three, or ten homes, or a whole city, or several cities agreed . . . to live in faith and love . . . even if no ordained man, shorn or anointed, ever came to them . . . Christ, without a doubt would be in their midst and would own them as his church.[11]

Would own them as his church! And his point? The priestliness of every household: "Every baptized Christian is . . . a priest."[12] "All Christians are priests. . . ."[13] ". . . the New Testament knows of no priest who is or can be anointed externally. . . . There is not a single word in Gospels or Epistles of the apostles in support of this vanity. . . . For a priest, especially in the New Testament, was not made but was born."[14]

When he is no longer able to preach and serve, *or if he no longer wants* to do so, he once more becomes a part of the common multitude of Christians. . . . The preaching office is no more than a public service which happens to be conferred upon someone by the entire congregation, all the members of which are priests.[15]

Did you hear that? He doesn't have to stay! His church is not tied to his office! The priesthood is not an *office*. It is a relation that permeates the whole body, each of whom is priest *to the neighbor*. My great teacher in this I first knew when he was a student in Baylor just out of the Air Force. Years later, he was my much loved associate at Austin. A while ago, in the middle of the night in Houston, I heard him tell me about his *new* church. It was twelve crippled, retarded children for whom he was the visiting public school teacher in the Houston system, and he had more church, he said, than he had when we "served" four thousand members! The church is in the priest, not vice versa! For the right and dignity of the priesthood remains *in communi* says Luther—*in the people.*[16]

And how does it work, the priesthood of the believer? *You, you,* take your priesthood wherever you are, to be whatever priests must be. There, where you and *they* are—you, all of you, *are the ministry of the Word.* This does not mean that you are competent to deal with God for yourself. It means rather that you are competent and responsible to deal with God and for the neighbor. It was a gross perversion of the gospel that inserted a bastard individualism here and then taught us that the believer's priesthood meant that "every tub must set on its own bottom." Instead of each of us looking to some hired hand who can step down when he wishes to, we priest each other. Yet, in tearing loose from your old dependency on your little Protestant Rome, says Luther, "as always you must reckon with a Cross."

The questions become: when will you assume your priesthood? When will you begin to ask for help in reversing the flow? When will you seek the Christian equipment you need to interpret the meaning of your calling, in your own situation, so that you can be a different priest from what we have had, before? Where do you begin? How do you as believer-priest get your training? How do you get competence to do your priesting? What happens to, what remains of, the institutional church? And what does this do to a full-time clergy? Can we get some kind of answer to these?

In the main, assuming our priesthood means no more "business as usual." We should have known this sixty years ago. We should have known this as early as the 1914 campaigns in World War I. It was evident from the way British Tommies regarded the chaplains who were with them that we could not go on with "business as usual." We haven't been "in business as usual" for a long generation. And this is a trouble to us all. Gibson Winter, in lectures at Duke, said that we are being called to radical changes in our forms of apostolate and ministry.[17]

The world around us is no longer a center of frontier individualism. It has become metropolitan. It has become pluralistic. It has become chaotic and overwhelmingly not-Christian. Those who can see this also see and say that the church is at least five times removed from the power centers of society. Ed Burnside, one of the great lay-priests who brought me to Charlotte, called this properly years ago when he claimed that the Chamber of Commerce had the real power there. I have put it in the phrase "the temple has always been downtown."

Those who see this have said that the church has to get out of the house. It has to get out of the house with millions of priests into a "new servanthood of the laity." Well and good, so far. But look!

The laity aren't ready—are you? We have used you for other purposes than the redemption of the world. We have been making you "props of virtue" on the front row for the offering's sake. We have let you help with the Supper. We have made you supports against the collapse of our half-supported institutions. And you

have been made to think that Christianity concerns events within the religious establishments . . . and have been given little or no help in discerning the theological dimensions of community development.[18]

Worse, pastors are incompetent and off-balance. We can't get in position for the grueling work, the close-up work, of influencing power structures at the sources of evil in society.

The direct influence of pastors upon community development becomes more and more difficult . . . the influence of Christianity on the residential environment . . . will have to be the work of laity who are familiar with the technical problems and engaged in the planning processes.

A laity who participate in the processes of society and develop theological sensitivity form the only possible Church in a mass society.[19]

The church you have known all your lives with its intensely dominant and active minister and a passively supporting laity is not God's people in the world; not anymore!

III

Our answer is not a "servanthood of the laity" as a nice addition to round out a hired professional staff; instead, what we are trying to say here is that the lay people must become *the ministry of the church in the world. It is* yours! This forces us to redefine everything! It is not that you as laymen are to pitch in and help out; it's that you are the only hope we have and this forces us to redefine everything! This *is* the ministry. It means we have to do *education* and *mission* and *evangelism* and *proclamation* and *witness* and *worship* and *stewardship* in a way that creates a "ministering laity in every public responsibility." Our task is not just to create mental, emotional health in the members. It is to proclaim and live hope, deliverance, and freedom amid the slaveries of our modern idolatry. This is Corinth and Ephesus and Athens and Rome all over. *The aim of the church is not to enlist its laymen in its services; the aim is to put laymen as theological competents in the service of the world!*

A startlingly apt support is the Scripture passage that begins, "And so [we came] to Rome" (Acts 28:14*b*, NEB). Rome, the metropolis, a sprawling morass of millions; fourteen wards would go up in smoke in this generation; it was a flea market of borrowed gods, a rabbit hutch of quick-bred hopes and leftover frustrations, a city of slaves and gold and intrigue. Here all the highways, all the power lines, all the sewers of the world ran together. Its Christian community had no clergy, no property, no power; it met in secret. *What will you do in Rome, Paul?* And more, *what will Rome do to you?* The answer was a house where a *competent layman, exposed to the things of God, reached for the most he could get, true to the tradition in which he had started; worked with what he got, receiving "all who came," in the context of the kingdom of God and the things concerning the Lord Jesus Christ.* And Paul "dwelled two years in his own house." This at least we could do, until there appears among us the prophetic fellowship on a journey that such priesting always calls forth.

Here our lives together could be a prophetic fellowship. The only budget question would be, "Does it help interpret?" The only curriculum question would be, "Does it make things clearer?" The only admission question would be, "Do you intend to be a pilgrim?" The only obligation would be that we should be priests to each other. That is to say, we, too, would be, like Bunyan's old layman,

sires of spiritual children, mothers of whole men and nurses, too. We would be "knowers of dark things" for sinners. We would be pleaders. We would be men who despise things present as men sure of a world to come.[20]

And the work of this prophetic fellowship? It would be the repairing of the damage; it would be *a great revolt against religion*. It would be the secularizing of the holy, through the witness to the values that remain among us, so that

    commissions, courts, and councils
      committees and divisions and departments
   banks, stores, universities,
     firms, corporations, directors

would be attended by men who know the Christian difference and act accordingly, as priests. Each of you has his priesthood.

In 1938 I was on my first church job for which anybody ever paid me anything. I was called by one of our fine contributors to assist in the rehabilitation of a drunk that he very much wanted well, because when sober he was worth thousands a year on the telephone, selling stuff. Sober he was great; drunk he stayed under the bed, and I attended him. I was young then and had lots of energy; I attended him. Drunk or sober, I attended him. But I failed utterly though I wore out the carpets in the old Homestead Hotel.

Years later I preached in the old place, and my former drunk was taking up the collection! He was a deacon! It had done no good for me to priest him! I was a hired hand who could do nothing. His boss had done it! He had learned to love him and live with him and save him. This is a proper priesting. And this put simply is what I am trying to say.

IV

There intrudes here the previous question about all these houses we've got on our hands. If we should succeed in emptying all our houses by turning us all into priests outside, what remains for the house to be? What becomes of the institution and its officers, functions, and responsibilities? As Paul once put it, "much in every way!" There remains all of what all those houses were indispensably and really for:

A COMMUNITY OF WITNESS

The Christian church is that community of witness which confesses Jesus Christ as Lord to the glory of God the Father. In confessing

Jesus who is the Christ as Lord of life, this community is united with all who confess his name, the whole church, living and dead. It includes, under the Holy Spirit, all that God has done, is doing, and will do. It reaches its fulfillment of faith and hope in its response to the life, the cross, and the resurrection of Jesus the Christ as the church which issues from the faithful confession of the same.

To God, the Father, the church is his creation and channel for his own achievement of his own purpose in history. To Christ, the church is his body, his necessary extension of himself, bearing Christ's person as the agent of God's love in and for the world. To the Holy Spirit, the church is the recipient of the Spirit's uniting, setting apart, empowering, and teaching activity which results in the church's effective, saving, enlightening witness in history (Ephesians).

THE CHURCH'S SETTING

This church, the very body of the Christ, is situated alongside, with, counter to, occupied by, and involved with this present time and place. The demand that confronts it is the redemption of the world, but according to Luther "the Word must do this thing and not us poor sinners." Even so, the church lives its life under "a sense of bounden duty and apostolic command" in the face of appalling contradiction from the world it is sent to save. In this world its position is one of humility, repentance, mercy, and sacrifice (like its Lord); and when it forsakes this attitude, its character as redeemer goes away in its enslavement by the powers of this present age. This church, as the "realm of redemption" (Robert Nelson), cannot get out of the world. It is the fellowship of the doomed who are being redeemed, but it is more: the church is the fellowship of those being redeemed who are becoming redeemers.

In this setting of church and world, as redeemer, the church, in a sense, is the conscience of the world, but only because it is responsible, more than any other, for knowing the higher way. This church lives wherever God's people are hearing and responding. This means that its first obligation may be the redemption of the church which is at "10th and Vine"—for its first word is the word against bad religion. It is the hearing and responding fellowship, not the institutional church, which has always been the conscience of our history.

In this time and place the church is more than conscience; it is also will: God's will to be and do, working in the world. This requires of it an obsession with the will of the Father and a radical obedience in the teeth of some things painful to face: war, race, poverty, education, the State, all orders of society and of creation; within them, and often counter to them, the church must live its life as conscience, will, and compassion.

THE CHURCH'S MEANS

As an instrument of God's Spirit, the church accomplishes its witness by several means: it worships, it preaches, it teaches, it has the cure of souls, and it has the vocation of its people. But it is the church which does these: the church worships; the church preaches and teaches, et cetera, however much it may use special men with special gifts for its work, and whether or not it knows various orders. Church is not church by virtue of its clergy. Church is church by virtue (unity and holiness) of its Lord!

In worship the whole of the church experiences the whole gospel in the whole of its life. Everything God is doing in creation, redemption, and consummation comes to bear here. And worship happens, or it does not happen, or it only seems to happen and so the church lives or dies or only seems to live. Here we (never I), the whole community of the faithful, come into the presence of God to adore, to confess, to give thanks, to proclaim and to hear, to respond and to partake. We are impressed by God's majesty and grace, our need for forgiveness in redemption; we are called to serve him; we make up our minds to serve him; and we go forth to obey. Here God is in his people at worship and at work. For the worship overspreads the work and *vice versa.*

In its preaching, since it is the church which preaches, the community is responsible for what it says and hears. It is God who has spoken and speaks in the church through men. The proclamation centers in an *agon* (the cross) and features an awareness of a desperate situation and a high hope. This proclamation is God's, who speaks in the church of what he is, does, and for whom he does this. But in church our preaching becomes of earth, earthy, for the church, too, has its earthen vessels. No one speaker has the answers; indeed, he may have naught but questions. The congregation answers (with mutters, or denial, or misunderstanding, or assent), and in the converse which is proclamation the whole church is involved in making persons while using its book, its minds, its converse, and its experiences in its Lord.

In its teaching the church experiences its faith played over the theme of doubt and insecurity. No church nurture is redemptive or relevant that forgets this. The means of witness that is education is a sequence of continual new exposures. The witness life in teaching is one of concerned, involved inquiry. The witness that is Christian nurture results in a race of people who have growing power over life and its a permeative factor of the church's life as natural as breathing. The witness becomes explicit in the power of maturing men, but what the church seeks to do is the same for those who are seven and those who are seventy. Through its demand for encounter and growth the church becomes a true church of God with a call to deliver; this is our vocation.

In its vocation the church is a *steward* and a *curer* of souls through the powers (gifts) of its people. The fiber of this witness is the stuff of its maturing people. The voluntary offering of self is all the church can give as fiber to its witness, for this is all we have. Summoned, we reply. The character of the reply is the character of our witness. Here the church receives or does not receive my work, family, worship, money, all things, and out of them fashions its hospitals, schools, books, and buildings.

Curers of souls. Here the church discovers its calling to be the total redemption of its whole world. Not all the church's lambs come up for feed and here we become burden bearers. This bearing of overloads— imposed burdens—is to be done wherever there are needs, in or out of the church. This is the life of the church-dispersed and is what true congregational life is all about.

THE CHURCH'S DIMENSIONS

In principle, we are saying, the church is a womb where God's kind of persons happen, are made, are called forth. This life in the church, of persons, is characterized by at least three dimensions: koinonia, diakonia, and leiturgia.

Life in the church is *koinonia* (fellowship) This is what we mean when we speak of persons as means of grace. We mean that we meet God in each other. When church is church, life is *koinonia*, both as church-gathered and as church-dispersed. Life is life in common wherever you are. *Koinonia* means to know as you are known: to be known utterly by one who calls you forth, whom you meet in the brother, before whom it is safe to come as you are. Wherever he is being made whole and well, a man is in church; wherever his burdens and need become my hunger and task, our wills merge and we hear God. *Koinonia* is not to have all things in common. It is to know each other in common. This is the sovereign grace of God in persons, that a man can be heard into the presence of the eternal and will never be able to be as if he had not been heard. This is salvation. Wherever the church forgets this hearing and being heard as the base of *Koinonia,* the structures it raises and serves work to our dissolution. Through this wicket gate of hearing, the door that is open and cannot be shut discloses a holy place.

There is also in the church the life of *diakonia, the service of obedient men.* Life in the church is the company of the obedient. Here in preaching which is teaching, teaching which is preaching, and in preaching-teaching which is dialogue and obedience, persons hear and obey and learn the church's ministry of mercy, the proper use of advantage and suffering, the cure of souls. Here the whole community becomes a ripener of souls and its obedience (stewardship) becomes a witness of the whole to the whole. In the life of obedience we are prepared for the discovery of a sacrament: that we are really dispensers of God's grace.

All these, then, who are aware of sin and need, fulfillment, and the need to praise; those who are aware of self and selves; those who are veterans of meeting with God—these come into the church. This church is the communion of the saints, the fellowship of believers, the way, the body of Christ, the communion of the Holy Spirit and his work; it finds its common experience, locale, conviction, effect, result, and its reason for being in the life, teaching, death, resurrection, and coming of Christ Jesus, unique Son of God and Savior of the world of men. All this is the dimension we call *leiturgia*, our liturgy, our worship-work-life.

This is why the church is like nothing else on the face of the earth; why it must never use the tools of the world for its gain; why it has to wait; why its members who are becoming persons have moral, ethical, relational, and personal obligations. This is why its fellowship is like nothing else you have tasted; and this is why its oneness is holiness, its baptism is a death, its bread is a strengthening, its wine is a toast to resurrection, the dust shaken off its feet is a testimony to God and those who have heard, and its failure is a sacrament. This is why we die without its renewal.

And now, here, in these last six pages, which took twenty years to write, I have said what the church is; but that is not the theme of this book. The real theme rests on our recovery of our most misused means: our *vocation* as stewards, curers, and priests.

In all of Luther's mighty works, *vocatio* (vocation), *calling*, if you please, never gets mixed up with office. The office one fills, as with Paul, rests upon the gift, gifts of the Spirit for administration, teaching, preaching, healing, etc. The calling is always the same thing, for all who hear and are hearers. He (Luther) hears Paul perfectly when Paul says, "I, Paul, call you along to the calling with which you are called" (Ephesians 4:1).

And pray what is our calling? Whatever the work *(Beruf)*, our calling is priesting-it-in-the-world. And here I cannot find a passage in Luther relevant to this matter that does not have in it the key word *"neighbor."* Over and over "the neighbor, the neighbor." The key is that in earth man is always bound to another, *in relatione.* This concept is utterly basic to any notion of community; but in Luther it is also always basic in ethics.[21] The theme of the neighbor followed through all of Luther's works would require hundreds if not thousands of references. And what does this mean? The most neglected basis for the church imaginable! *Priest at my elbow is of the essence! We are priests to each other.*

I do not priest me. I priest *you* and vice versa. On this the community of witness takes its rise. Without it no church exists at all.

V

But this is all preliminary to my purpose. Having said this, as primal, foundational, absolutely basic, the task now is to make some contribution to your equipage for priesting it in the world. For the church's obligation to you in its teaching office is at least this: to equip the priest for his service-work as priest in *this* world. As Luther puts it, priesting *is* for this world, for in the next world our work is of no consequence. Salvation really is by faith and grace.

As the only priest there is, then, would it help you to know that you really do have something to put your weight on? Would it give you heart for the task to know for sure that we Christians have at our disposal a mighty secret; and would it help you to know what that secret is? This is the intention for chapter 1, "The Christian Genius."

As only priest, would it help if someone broke down for you the real meaning of faith and showed you how its only concern is with the "*I am,*" the *being* of a person, and how we miss that if we keep getting tied up with the substitutes this life offers us? That is the goal for chapter 2, "The Grammar of Faith."

As priest in this world only, can you stand the strain of the honest attempt to see the unbelievable distortion of form and shape the church has been put through by our centuries old and recent use of bad structural models; and would you be willing to risk the changes and conflicts that "The Christian Genius" and "The Grammar of Faith" call for in such a setting and time as ours? This is the attempt I am making in chapter 3, "The Recovery of Form and Shape."

We turn a big corner in chapter 4. Here the concern is to put down a way for Christian adults to come to accept the demand upon us priests to submit to the correction of our images by the Christ. Where, how, at what cost, and with what grace this happens is an approach to Christian education that promises full humanity as a prospect—if only we can find "The Nerve to Submit."

All this means that priests, only priests, can never be strangers to change and conflict. How we find conflict a means to communion and change a door to the redemption of the whole world is the theme of two chapters: "Conflict and Tension"; "Change and Revolution." Added up, the total is a hope for the priest at my elbow, for us priests to each other, for here is our experience of revelation.

What if the Christian meaning rests on a broad ledge of truth and insight that is from four to twenty thousand years older than the Christian gospel? And what if the Christian gospel is the crucial acting out in history of an insight so profoundly true that the whole history of civilization is a supporting demonstration? If this were so, and you could know about it, would it not give you such confidence in your calling as a Christian that you could risk everything? We Christians have a secret truth now so obvious as to stun us that we ever doubted it.

1

THE CHRISTIAN GENIUS

It is a very great thing—after a long dry spell, when your ideas are so shriveled that you begin to suspect the futility of the whole modern journey; all institutions seem suspect to you, all values moldy; and the work of your life is threatened with meaninglessness—to come across a sudden and great justification that sends you back to the wars.

It is a very humbling, even humiliating, thing suddenly to discover, years after you had published, that your most serious attempt *and* a fundamental judgment your work rests on now need radical correction.[1] It is embarrassing to confess that you had suspected this, had tried to allow for it, but had not taken your hunch seriously enough. (Anyone who is operating theologically as he did fifteen years ago is probably inept and irrelevant.) However, if you admit this need for correction, it may mean a break through your own crust to some primal ground. It will be a chance to modify an error, and it may very well be your discovery of a meaning the gospel always had. At any rate, it is a very precious thing to come suddenly upon a lever with hooks to turn things over so that you can *see.* The Christian faith becomes in such a moment a fantastic acting out of a decision made millennia before.

Somewhere, sometime, by somebody or bodies who mattered, a

decision was taken seriously between two fundamental options. A direction was established. A fundamental point of view became the mode of existence for enough peoples and tribes to create a cultural orientation, a "principle of cohesion," a ground of being. *It is the most important decision in the history of the world.*[2] Everything in the West is derived from this decision. I have no notion whatever who made it, but everything that is Western depends upon it and everything that is now truly Eastern contrasts with it. It marks all of Western life: philosophy, art, architecture, communal life, economics, politics, and religion. Every single aspect of life reflects it and even the Eastern ideas, tools, and vast heritage that remain alive in the West are alive because they contributed to and participated in this decision.

It was *the decision to get into this world.* Every fundamental inquiry on the nature of things begins here. Every real East-West difference rises here. It now seems to be the key to a so-called Western civilization. Everything proceeds from this decision, and the East must eventually come to terms with it. For this is the real determinant that has put the West in such Eastern places as China, Japan, Korea, and Vietnam. We cannot refuse to be Western and live. This would be to try to revoke twenty thousand years of history's determined pressure to abhor a vacuum just as nature does.

THE DECISION TO RISK IT

In none of my earlier work did I make sufficient allowance for the weight and size of this primal Western decision about matter. In my anxiety to get out of materialism which, says Kant, shatters on the humblest earthworm, I had nearly missed *that materialism without which no Western world is possible and with which no real secularism is conceivable.*

Our ancestors raised two questions. What is man? What is this cosmos? The Western world is a cohesive and historical whole because it everywhere says the two questions have one answer: *Whatever man is can be discovered only by man's involvement with the stuff of this present place and time.* Western man literally dove into matter. He exploded out of the Garden of Eden with a hammer in his hand. He hammered, twisted, melted, congealed, braided, shaped, organized, traded, harnessed, mastered the stuff of this present world. The secret of the Western man is the passion with which he sank into matter at whatever risk to Spirit. The West went on a venture, a journey, finding its banners as it went and fighting always its nostalgia to go East and out of this world. It has no indisputable starting point. Fire, wheel, stirrup, plow: all are incidents of the journey into matter. And out of the journey, says De Rougemont, the West has produced alone the first two answers to its question: Man is *person;* cosmos (order) means *machines.* But the answers come at considerable risk.

For man came out of Eden both guilty and anxious. He had sinned against Spirit, and this made for guilt. He had risked the loss of Spirit, and this made him anxious. Over his shoulder he had to decide "What shall I do about Spirit? Abandon?" But to his consternation he discovered that Spirit would not abandon him! In his guilt and anxiety he had still his fundamental concerns. What of the self? Is it real or illusory? And what of matter? Is it good or bad? And yet he retained a confidence in Spirit that sustained him on some days. His anxiety has always been that he would go so far from the Garden of Eden he would smother in the stuff that attracted him. He might get so far from Spirit that he would swamp his little boat.

Every Christian thinker of the first six centuries goes to his knees on the horns of this dilemma. Augustine agonized from boyhood through his late twenties before he escaped his Manichaean phase.[3] The two questions are: what about matter and what about the self— cosmos and man? For each it was a venture anew. We cannot find the starting point—wheel, stirrup, or whatnot. All over the East, matter was evil and a prison for the soul. You cannot find the West's first resolve to run the risk of playing with fire—but here we are—and still playing with fire. No starting point is found, but you can very easily find its center. For without some true center the West could not have endured the risk and would have gone back into the Nirvana of Spirit in the absence of matter. That answer is obvious to the eye and mind but is not totally without its risks as well.

INCARNATION

With respect to this startling answer to the question about Spirit and matter, Denis De Rougemont is still the teacher. He, first, for me, had nerve to give matter its proper place in the meaning of the West: he opens with this question.

What human attitude is presupposed by Western civilization which has made its most typical creations possible? And he answers: *a fundamental anxiety* at the creation of risks that constantly call previous securities to question. In its anxiety over and obsession with matter the West came out with *persons* and *machines*. The underlying attitude is revealed in the fundamental options: what to do with matter (good or bad); and what to do with the self (illusory or real). The answers shape the civilization!

The West arose "like a venture." De Rougemont thinks it really was under way only "out of a most unwonted and hardly credible event which supervened at the hazardous crossroads of diverse traditions, some of them incompatible." [4] This initiating shock, this personification, this appearing, in point of truth, is *Incarnation, the greatest idea in our history of the world!*

Incarnation is the cant hook the West has found and has been found by. With this hook we turn over our universe. But this judgment is premature and from here seems precocious, even immature. For incarnation is not a primal idea but is derivative, likely arrived at experientially; and its name and nature can be seen only after the journey is farther along. The really great decision—to run the risk of plunging into matter—and our permanent direction for thousands of years behind us—came far ahead of the verbalization of any notion of incarnation.

The East was dawn, light, sun, spirit. In that direction the way leads out of this world. The West was twilight, dark, foreboding, a place of matter and dragons. In that direction lay the edge of the world, too. And the risk and anxiety are still there. But as we look back toward, and are driven back on, our origins, we come across an inescapable personification of manhood that is immense in human-divine implications. Two thousand years later we are finding tools to explain it. We can now see, fourteen hundred years later, what all the six centuries of debate about *persons* in the Trinity was really about.[5] We can now read our own Middle Ages as no Dark Age, but a determinative sloughing off of a perennial demand to turn back East and out of this world. And we can now see both the promise and the threat in the tools with which we have handled this world: *science, industry, business,* and *government.*

The threat? Still the same threat: we may smother in the stuff and be lost. The promise? The resolution of the contradiction in an incarnation where matter and spirit are one.

The content of our drama is that *it happened once.* This is the basis of our preachment. Incarnation as the answer to the matter-spirit risk was acted out. And the Word (not silence)

was made *flesh* (not concept)
   and *grace* (not merit)
     ministered to faith (not knowledge)
      in such a way that person (not individual)
       will act as though he were an incarnation, too.

                    (See John 1:14, 16.)

Incarnation is our answer. It says that matter is neither good nor bad; that the real question is the self who is involved with a material creation. Matter as created is a stuff with which the Creator is pleased. Use it with the self that is real, not illusory. You may neither transcend nor otherwise escape the self and its stuff. You may deprive the self, choke and deny the self for stuff; or you may free and be freed. This is the creative action of the Son of God in flesh, but this incarnation serves to demand *other* incarnations and here the risk is both personal and terrible.

We are being forced back on our origins, says Ruth Nanda Anshen. We are in difficult times. The self in its radical freedom may drown in a surfeit of stuff or its own Nirvana. We must realize either the material or the spiritual or both. Whether you wish it so or not, our present place is not one we can abandon. If Word is Word for you, it must be Word in your flesh, too, and this is the risk: Every incarnation risks a drowning! Either you will smother in the stuff of this present human existence, or you will know a triumph of the self through matter.

The decision to risk this present world is the invitation to submit to a great diversion—to lose, perchance, the self in the sack of things the self uses. And here, the example of our elders is, as elsewhere, not so good.

The threat, in part, is that we did not get done with incarnation. One of these will never do. Every self is an incarnation, in prospect, and this is too much. The threat is not just a failure with matter, it is a failure of the self to happen—to come into its incarnation, too. The very capacity of our fingers for manipulation is a threat. The stuff turns over on us and we drown:

the peddler becomes a merchant, then a prince-tycoon;
but ends with no self.
the pilgrim becomes a tribesman, then a politico;
and sacrifices the self.
the creator becomes mere manipulator; and
the self disappears in its fleshy dress.

Relation is absorbed in function or never happens. Person is cut off in individual. Dynamic is static and the fluidity of potential is turned into vested deposits. Man equals $'s—or he is man only if he has stuff. Yet the way to manhood is still through material seas, and we have to risk that flesh may win.

Against this triumph of the flesh there is an impressive biblical witness: "Let those who live in the world not mix in the world" (1 Corinthians 7:31); "All things are lawful; not all are expedient" (1 Corinthians 6:12; 10:23); "nothing unclean of itself" (Romans 14:14; see also 1 Corinthians 8:9; 10:25f.; 1 Timothy 4:4); "you have been called into liberty, only use not liberty for an occasion to the flesh; but by love serve one another" (Galatians 5:13); "All things are yours . . . and you are Christ's, and Christ is God's" (1 Corinthians 3:21, 23, RSV).

"Love God and do what you will," says Augustine, and everyone else, but only Augustine adds and asks, "What do I love when I love my God?" The terrible potential for this incarnation of ours is encased best in Romans 1. Regardless of our example, we already know and have this situation:

all that may be known of God you know already, for God has showed it to you. He has made clearly available to you all the powers of himself and you can understand them through material *made-things,* even his power and personhood. Incarnation is all around—permeation is everywhere—but there are no guarantees. This information assures nothing. To know about your godhood is not to glorify or demonstrate it. You may choose to be not thankful, but vain, foolish, and darkened; you may fall for an idol of creeping things and God will go away leaving you to be embalmed by the odors of your own flesh. The threat is that you may mistake creature for Creator and thus turn public truth to private lie, for to be inexcusable is to be responsible (Romans 1:19-25).

The just lives in this by faith—no other world, way, or weapon.

> A man of faith is bound to be a man on his way, a viator, the eternal "sojourner on earth," who has here below "no abiding city." He knows not; he believes. He has not; he hopes for. He sees not; he obeys. And his road is not defined like the unvarying orbit of a star, but is permanently venture; it is created under the feet of those who take it.[6]

Faith here becomes "active confidence" living "essential anxiety."

The Christian drama: it was acted out once; it got in our history as the starting point of a journey we were already taking. Advent—He came; ascension—He went away; amazingly—He stayed among us.

Around the country stores, churches, and schools of the Delta country in Mississippi, for several years, a huge overalled Negro man (who had earned a master's degree from Harvard) would just appear, talk to a collation of field hands until a few heard what he knew about manhood and freedom; then he would go away, change his name, and—.

If you were one of those whose freedom hope was your own manhood, wouldn't you call his going away an ascension? And wouldn't you keep looking for him everywhere? That would be an incarnation in your experience.

THE GENIUS

I would not want you to think that I think that if you see and say what I have seen and said that your saying will make any particular difference. I cannot see that my saying has mattered much. I only want you to see that we *do* have something still to stand upon—incarnation—for all of us. It is there whether we see or say.

Nor would I want you to think that I am naive enough to think the

West knows its base, or that the West is Christian. The West had already, before the shock of incarnation, powerful chemicals cooking in its retort—Greek views of man, for example.[7] (Karl Menninger wrote that he was going to Greece in the summer—he wanted to know why Greek ideas of man got no further than they did, and why Zeus gave us *destructiveness* as our birthright for choosing to play with fire.) The West also was getting a notion of Roman *order;*[8] it would come upon German tribal notions of freedom (vrai-doom). It was already a depository for Eastern traditions that go far, far behind the Jewish genius and contribute to both Jew and Greek. And, the West had already the fundament of Jewish Oneness.[9] All these in the same brewing cultural cauldron make for a potent ferment.

Rougemont insists that it was, however, the shock of Christian incarnation, with the whole of the previously stirring ferment, that really sparked *man's Western quest.* The Christian elements were sometimes utterly damaged, he says, but they were always *decisive* and *axial* in the quest. We can afford to be bold about that. For there is a Christian genius which survives any perversion of our two master ambitions: to know the secret of man and the secrets of the cosmos. In this quest we are no less involved than any contemporary astronaut.

Many of our contemporaries who stay in some so-called Christian ministry or other lose this genius or have never found it. It seems so easy for them to eke out their lives holding to some substitute for the genius of the faith that it is small wonder we shudder and turn away, fearing to be like them. (How different most of us are at forty-eight from what we were at twenty-eight!)

This Christian genius is not the Christian organizational schemes so many use as career refuge and defense. In its organization the church has always reflected its surrounding culture.[10] Most ranks and many clergy titles are a reflection of power grades within the Roman Empire, while German feudalism and British class structures have furnished many "Christian" assemblies their model. For that matter, do you know any single thing more expressive of American organized Christianity than the tools, titles, and structures we have taken from the American business community? This is not our genius—no matter how we tinker with the chassis.

Nor is the Christian genius reflected in our political schema. The faith has lived vigorously under all of these schemes: tyranny, oligarchy, monarchy, democracy, socialism, fascism, and communism. It is just not true that Christianity can survive only with democracy. Democracy is a latecomer that has never yet arrived, and this is not our genius though that genius, lived with, may produce something very like democracy as a way of life.

Bluntly, too, let us admit that the Christian genius is not our idea of incarnation. Though everything really important in the Christian faith depends upon incarnation, it is not exclusively our own. Others have used the idea of incarnation. (I have traced nineteen dying and rising gods in the Mediterranean world alone.) The Greek gods came down among men. The Hindu *avator* means that the divine descends into an animal or a man. Hindus claim ten incarnations of Vishna, of which Gautama Buddha is numbered *nine*. The tenth of the incarnations (Kalki) will destroy our degenerate world. In Hindu thought, God is incarnated whenever the scales seem to tip toward the triumph of evil. This means that such incarnation is all myth and no history, except for the stories of Buddha. But even if our incarnation really is "once for all" and dated when Caesar took a census, even if our genius derives from such an incarnation (time and place), we have still to say what the Christian genius may be.

The Christian genius is not even our thought about God. This is *Jewish* and great. Our real genius is *the Christian notion of man.*

Here in this framework we can afford to speak. No other frame permits all we can learn and say of man in all our disciplines of inquiry to be so meaningful. Mircea Eliade is right when he says that Christianity *really is the religion of modern man and of fallen man.*[11] In no other tongue can he (man) be so fully and truly described. Under no other rubrics can man be so well understood; and nowhere, nowhere else, has he the potential the Christian faith can claim. This is our genius: our notions of man.

Here we are veterans of a 2,000-year journey and fight. (As late as Schleiermacher, a century and a half ago, we still could not speak properly of persons, which may be why his God never became person.)[12] The fight toward personhood was great in its beginnings.

Paul's letters could have told us our true genius much earlier, but we were diverted by conciliar cleavages where the debate was God's Personhood, though the issue, hidden from all eyes in the Six General Councils, was man as *person*.[13] Off the main stem of developing personhood, Greek "individuals" filtered through the centuries into Roman "citizens" which resulted in rampant individualism. But the real ferment rested on an earlier debacle. The barbarians could not be stopped, but some of them fell into the Roman tide and absorbed the Christian base for persons, centuries flowing underground.[14] All that debate about the Personhood of God, it now turns out, was really about man and the neighbor where God appears to us, and this is the Christian difference. What the Greeks meant by *individual* and what we Christians mean by *person* are two different things entirely.[15]

The individual is the self with its things. The person is the self with the selves who created and called him out. This is Christian community. No human being who wishes to be *person* can any longer be individual. This is the meaning of Trinity—God in his social relations.[16]

Applied to man in the New Testament, the Christian genius produces the most amazing claim to greatness for man in world literature. We have been centuries coming to understand that we really do have a secret—"the secret truth" about man. We know you, who you are. You are an incarnation, too, whether you know it or not. This is our secret. We know who we are, and who you are, and it is god-like. The New Testament spills the secret on every page. We can afford to talk about man—who he is:

When the Comforter comes, he will show you. . . . All may be one, as thou, Father, art in me. . . . All things are yours, and you are Christ's, and Christ is God's . . . the promise is to you and to your children. . . . All creation stands on its tiptoes to see the maturing of the sons of God. . . . All things are for your sakes . . . if any man be in Christ he is a new creation. . . . (See John 15:26; 17:21; 1 Corinthians 3:21, 23; Acts 2:39; Romans 8:19; 2 Corinthians 5:17.)

. . . that Christ may dwell in your hearts through faith; that you, being rooted and grounded in love, may have power to comprehend with all the saints what is the breadth and length and height and depth, and to know the love of Christ which surpasses knowledge, that you may be filled with all the fulness of God (Ephesians 3:17-19).

If we see and say this secret about man, who he really is, we can still talk. My great teacher, William Owen Carver, was obsessed fifty years with the Ephesian epistle, and he called that last phrase "the most supernal insight into man's real nature in our history." The aging Karl Barth saw this, too and wrote near his end the stunningly beautiful little essay, "The Humanity of God"![17]

We have a genius, we Christians, and it is something about man.

In the Christian way, the word *faith* is always a verb! There really is no single word in English which says well the meaning of that verb; closest perhaps would be "to believe-obey." When we make faith into a noun, we freeze it into a creed! It really is a verb!

Now don't let this put you off! There's hardly a word in this chapter that you did not learn in your sixth grade English grammar!

The life of obedience-in-trust, believing-obeying, the faith-life, is lived out principally in our use of the verbs: *to have, to do, to be,* but the primal verb is the verb *"to be."* All "faithing-it" is expressible in

I am, you are, he is,
We are, you are, they are,

with all the other forms, tenses, and moods that make up the English irregular verb.

But look, once, when I was pressing this meaning upon a group of bishops and leaders at Laity Lodge, a very keen lay-theologian and linguist, Betty Mann, brought this forward: The more regular a verb in its forms and conjugation, the later it is in the language, and, conversely, the more irregular the verb, the *earlier* it is. All the way back to Sanskrit, said Betty Mann, the *most* irregular of verbs is the verb "to be."

It must be positively primal, first, of the essence of existence. What if that is all that Christian faith is really about? It's something about *Being*.

2

THE GRAMMAR OF FAITH

If we do not see it and say it—our secret truth about man—we cannot stay in these old mausoleums which the half-read faith of our ancestors built. And, to see and say may take us outdoors anyhow. But we cannot talk at all unless we see and say the secret truth of man: How shall we escape if we neglect the genius?

In a remarkable little book, *From State Church to Pluralism,*[1] Franklin Littell has called the U.S.A. the greatest mission field in the world. In the first of three current studies of the church in metropolis, Gibson Winter lamented *The Suburban Captivity of the Churches.* Frank Littell means that in the main we are but third-generation Christians. (There are older Christian communities in China.) We have barely begun to exploit the meaning of the gospel; our great work is still here. Winter means that already, in spite of an astounding statistical success, Christianity as religion has been removed to, established in, and limited by the bedroom communities that serve the service centers of the nation. Here Christianity loses its bite and becomes a possession and an obligation, not a vital being as man. Both are right. We *are* a mission and needy field; we are already decadent!

We cannot come at this from modern pulpits with *nouns*. Words, nouns, the names of things, such as *church, God, salvation*, always wind up in the dative case as a means to our end, or in the accusative case as direct objects for our benefit. We have to get at *persons* with the verbs, the primal verbs. All of our eternals and the genius we may at times communicate depend for their communication on the *verbs*. The vitality of our faith is its *grammar. Salvation by grace* is *the* nominative clause, the subject of the Christian promise, but we have to talk about it with the verbs, not the adjectives we have used to make it pretty. And here our prime weakness is manifest. We have allowed all our primal verbs to be heard as *intransitive* verbs: they all take direct objects for our benefit! *The meaning of salvation by grace is that all our primal verbs are always transitive: "to have," "to do,"* and *"to be" can never take a direct object and be Christian verbs*. This is the point of our manhood in grace: we *have* no-thing, we *do* no-thing, we *are* no-thing in order to *be* no-particular-thing. Our having, doing, and being have their point in themselves! Thus man can only appear as who he is with God. Let me show you what I mean: I mean to come at our manhood through a proper limitation to the transitive of our primal verbs: to have, to do, to be.

TO HAVE, TO DO, TO BE

Everywhere I know us Christians well, Christianity is something one "has." To be Christian is "to have religion." It is a possession, a label one wears to show his brand or kind. It is something that *comes* to one, a given which, once he has got it, settles things. Christianity is answers. Christianity is divine connections. It is a passage paid one way, subject only to a seasonal renewal. To have religion is to be secure. It is a "not having to ask questions." It's an armor one wears: a map, a policy, a catalog, a warranty deed promising delivery.

I kept for one week the questions I heard raised in my own parish out of a context where religion is something one *has:*

"Why cannot Christianity be a very simple thing?"

"My father never concerned himself with all these questions, he had religion!"

"Religion is so much more complicated than it used to be."

"What sort of kick are they on down there now?"

"What is all this business of *concern* about people? Why can't everyone have it just like I've got it?"

"I don't like a religion that gets all involved with questions and issues."

"For me, religion is a very simple thing and ought to stay in its place."

"Why is it my children spurn so what I think about religion? Why don't they accept just as I did?"

"Why does that fellow we hired make it sound so hard?"

"Religion is good fellowship. It's everybody knowing everybody. It's a good feeling you get on the Sundays you go. It's an uncomplicated bed into which one crawls as a child and to which he keeps returning to be sure Mother is still there."

"I don't understand all this disturbance. I just accept! I like the old songs, simple stories, Bible faith. David never had these problems and Jesus didn't talk about them!"

"You've either got it or you haven't, and if you've got it, you've got it. My Mother had a very simple faith and if I could just be the Christian she was!"

"I just take the Bible on faith. You know I have no idea what they are talking about in that class."

"Do you *know* what "they" are teaching those children? I understand we have teachers who do not believe in the virgin birth. Is that so?"

"I never really liked to read. Why so much emphasis on this? Religion just means trusting God!"

Then the man who "has religion" walks into a trap. He finds himself in a setting where nothing he says, thinks, or has, matters. He is utterly bewildered by the conversation around him; someone hands him a *book*. Perhaps it is one of the older and great theological paperbacks of the time: Arthur Miller's, *Death of a Salesman,* or *On The Beach* (Nevil Shute); John Updike's great third novel, *Rabbit, Run,* (I am Rabbit's pastor some days), or one of Lawrence Durrell's *Quartet,* or even William Golding's *Lord of the Flies,* or J. D.

Salinger's *Catcher in the Rye,* or Tennessee Williams' prize *Cat on a Hot Tin Roof,* or part I, especially, of William Faulkner's *The Sound and the Fury,* or Jean Sartre's *No Exit;* or if he is a Southerner, Sartre's *The Respectful Prostitute,* or Albert Camus' *Rebel,* Franz Kafka's *Trial;* or still the greatest, T.S. Eliot's *The Wasteland.*

Perhaps someone hands him, in the seventies, some great piece of more recent vintage: *Catch 22, Portnoy's Complaint,* or the reissued *Streetcar Named Desire, Exodus,* or Philip Roth's *The Breast,* or one of the great contemporary Russians; or most threatening of all to a naive notion of man, the incredible short stories of Flannery O'Conner. He can't "cut" any of them. They are gobbledegook to him. As a matter of cold fact, he got lost right after *Girl of the Limberlost* or *Tom Swift and His Electric Locomotive.* It is not that he is stupid or unintelligent. He just fell out of the world and got lost. The world, and religion, is filled with a language he does not know. For him, religion wasn't supposed to matter much, it was something he already had or something he could get if he needed it during some illness.

Are you saying, Mister, that Christianity is a matter of having a library card, belonging to a book club, or running back and forth to a paperback book store? Are you saying, Mister, that to be Christian is to be hep, not square, but cool, not offended by pornography? Are you saying that to be Christian is to be current?

One can have read everything from Irving Stone's *The Agony and the Ecstasy* or his *The Passions of the Mind,* back to the 1916 version of *Uncle Billy's Whiz Bangs* and still not have caught the force, the storm, of theological relevance and concern that sweeps the modern stage, novel, poetry, essay, photographic arts, much less the plastic, active, and still-art forms. To have said that to be Christian is to be *hep* would be simply another gnosticism, and we have plenty of that. It would be as foolish as to say that sewing is done in sewing clubs, or that garden-club members make gardens. It would be like saying the Christian faith is in the church!

It is as bad to say Christianity is something one *knows* as to say Christianity is something one *has,* or something he *does.* The Christian faith is someone one *is.* Against the backdrop of this concern I kept a second list of questions heard that same week. They give witness to the existence of another very human country:

"Am I losing my mind?"

"Why does absolutely no one love me?"

"What can I do to make Someone, anyone, hear?"

"If all this I see is true about me, how do I begin?"

"In the face of all I've given her, what does she mean when she says I never heard or understood anybody?"

"Why did my Daddy die and do me this way?"

"Why did that man make me a *thing?*"

"Why does your church reject the man who needs it most?"

"How far do you go with a man who will not give *any*thing?"

"How long can one wait for redemption to begin?"

"What do you mean when you say there are rooms upstairs?"

"Why do my children spurn everything I love?"

"What can I do to be saved from this splitness?"

"To whom can I turn over all my responsibility?"

And a seminarian, a new B.D. from up-East asks, "What will really fill my hollow heart?" These are the novels a journeyman pastor has read to him. This is the context out of which he speaks, if he speaks, on Sunday. He listens seven days to pay for his privilege of talking twenty minutes. What he says can abide, if he knows that faith means not having or doing, but being Someone one *is*.

One day our Lord came to the little hill home of Lazarus and his sisters. The church remembered that he had said to much busied Martha, "One dish is enough for a meal!" (See Luke 10:42*a*.)

One day Jesus was overtaken on a journey by a well-off young patrician who queried, "What must I *do* to inherit eternal life?" (See Matthew 19:16-22.) The church remembered that Jesus dealt with him in terms of the disposition of what he *had,* so that he might come to terms with *being*.

There was a man of the Pharisees, named Nicodemus, a leader of the Jews. He came to Jesus by night and asked what he must *do* to merit eternal life (John 3:1-21). The church remembered that Jesus refused to deal with him on this level and led Nicodemus to talk of birth—and *being*.

This is the point of the church's memory about the visit to the home of Simon, the Pharisee (Luke 7:40-44). There was a street-woman there who was closer to *being* than Simon could be. The point about doing was disposed of again in the parable of the farmer and the workers who were paid the same, even though some began as late as four in the afternoon (Matthew 20:1-16).

As for Paul, who notoriously had less patience over this having-doing syndrome, he simply says, in the flaming Galatian epistle: "I wish all those who keep calling for circumcision, circumcision, would cut the whole thing off!" (Galatians 5:12.)[2] Holy Scripture is filled with understanding that *religion is more* than something one has or does. The dullest faith there is rises in *doing* things. The only religion poorer than a merely *doing* religion is one based on *not doing* things. And what a reputation some of us have for this!

> Baptists are the people who don't drink with their friends! Methodists are the people whose schools are built with tobacco, but whose pastors must not smoke.

John the Baptizer came, not eating, not drinking, not socializing; Jesus came eating, drinking, and consorting with publicans (whatever *they* were). (See Matthew 11:18f.) Neither was what he was because of what he *did:* nor are we.

In all levels of Christian faith there is a proper action. What is it proper to do? Religious doing that matters endures only as it rises out of faith-being. *Action* never substitutes for *Being* though it manifests being. Church is happening anywhere that what I do and what I am come together worthily. Worship is work; fellowship is witness; proclamation *is* action; and challenge is response. But there is more.

AFFIRMATION OF BEING

The rabbi begins, "Thus saith the *Lord!"* The priest begins, "As the *Church* has always said. . . ." The average Protestant begins, "Now, brethren, it seems to *me*. . . ." This story was told as a joke at a meeting of Jewish-Christian Church-Synagogue administrators in Miami. But I take it as a serious distinction! This is legitimate. The Protestant affirms his being, his selfhood. For it matters as to what "it" seems to him. It is the thrust of his "I am."

The child asserts himself by declaring "I am" in various ways. He interrupts his elders; he explores premises; he handles forbidden gimcracks in his aunt's parlor; he reaches for things. The adult, threatened by his own nonbeing, affirms himself the same way, with what he can get, and with what he does.

Who cannot confirm or deny himself on the basis of what he has or does not have? This is easy, obvious, and prevalent. When I look at what I have or should have by now, I am comforted or disturbed. A little piece of land and some trees, part of a house or two, a share or so of stock, and the people I daily use: they are affirmations of *me*.

The owners of a nearby drive-in had the first and last syllables of their separate names put together and spelled out: *Marney's,* in neon letters three feet high! I took my real, though vicarious, kicks from this and was credited over the neighborhood with great business acumen, until some teenagers full of beer broke up the place. Then I disowned it quickly enough.

This was the appeal of fishtail fenders on old Cadillacs, of cutouts on hotrods, of squirrel tails on jalopies. This is the display of the newly rich, and this is the appeal of the ownership of gadgets to the never rich.

As we rode past a mountain cabin, outside littered with refuse and scrap, no window glass, no lawn, no bread in the house likely, both horses bolted at the explosion to life of a power mower. "My Lord, what a salesman!" my riding companion offered. But it was simpler than that. For a man who had no electricity, television, or even plumbing, the mower was his extension of himself into modernity.

It's the same with the latest fashions, new hairdos, and green makeup. This is why a girl's first high heels are so important. They are the extension of her being into maturity. Possession is an extension of *me*. Boats, trailers, leashed exotic dogs, wigs, or bank stock, it's all the same.

I first became acutely aware of this in a Japanese orphanage years ago when Father Chichetti opened the flimsy little bureau drawers for me to see that no matter what their racial origin, little derelicts of war with sores on their heads save tobacco tins, shiny rocks, string, marbles, tops, and old dried frogs; these are extensions of a little boy's existence. Once Mother was showing me something she had kept, and from the box there fell old Boy Scout registration cards and badges from forty years before. She was keeping something we had had. It was an old affirmation of a treasured existence. It was memory of a possession that was affirmation of being, past tense. Here in this old room where I work, I look up to see guns I no longer wish to shoot, pipes I never smoke, books I have not read, notes I once made in class, boots I have no time to wear, with posted souvenirs of the longer journeys. These are meaning of my existence extended. I keep them to affirm me. *To be is to have.*

For most people religion is that possession which affirms us before God. It affirms that we are a people with *character.* Religion is something I have. To have is transitive; it takes a direct object. I have "a holy feeling," or a set of vague ideas, or a code. I have a list of don't-dos, a set of morals. Religion which I have is a hand in a game I play; it is a face one wears, a reaction one makes, a garment he puts on. To be religious is to have religion, while church is a possession one is obligated by his ownership to preserve, keep up, operate well, much like one's garage must be kept clean, or his attic is an obligation. To have religion affirms us before God as God's kind. But there is more to this misuse of transitive verbs.

Who is not also affirming his being with *what he does?* To be is to do; to be is what I do. What I do is an extension of me. Indeed, do I not do in order to be? My doing reveals me. What I do affirms me to myself and my fellows as certainly as what I have: Boy Scout merit badges, the hash marks on a sailor's sleeve, the list of my connections and offices, the obituary sketch sent ahead for some stranger to introduce me by everywhere I go to make a speech. All this evidence that I have *done* is to affirm my present existence.

What I do to destroy is an affirmation of me—even a negative. The rages, denials, rejections, hostilities, and aggressions—all are to affirm me; they are my *power.* What I do to construct is an affirmation of me. All my joinings, supporting, striving, building, making, selling—indeed, I do in order to demonstrate to myself, and others, that I am.

To be religious involves what I do with what I have. False as this is, literally, there is something to this. Doing and having are inescapable *functions* of being, but they are not being. And they are results, effects, of being, not supports of being. Our religious doing and having rests on our being, not otherwise. In whatever year we are now in our experiment in faith, where would we be without the doings that have been done and the havings that have been had and given? But also, where are we sure enough in any way that matters unless these doings and havings rest on our being—our "isness?"

The Christian faith rests on neither doing nor having. Salvation by faith is salvation by grace—an affirmation of being as being. It means a willingness to be as one is without any direct object. He is as he is, warts and all. To be is to be whether one is sick or well, crippled, dumb, blind, or rich. To be is to be, even without arms and legs; one could almost say without mind. To be is to be without defense, possession, excuse, power, energy, or will. It is never to be *what.* The objects all drop off. We are stripped—no harness, no titles, no havings, no gotness, no doings. Being is just being. And this is where Christ meets me—just as I am.

"While we were yet sinners, Christ died for . . ." (Romans 5:8, RSV).

"In due time . . ." (Galatians 4:4).

"Yea, though you are newborn in your afterbirth . . .
and abandoned . . ." (Ezekiel 16:6).

By and large you have been hiding behind your having and doing; you know you have misused these verbs, and most of us have missed the point. A teenaged paraplegic, who has no hands or legs to use, little voice, no way to be mobile, and really almost nothing but a mind, asked by some ill-made social worker if she wouldn't as soon be done with it all, answers: "I wouldn't have missed being for anything." Some days here I laugh about Harry Denman, known particularly for his Spartan disdain for possessions, held up for hours in San Francisco, searched by customs people because all he had to show for his six weeks in the Orient was a paper bag with a toothbrush, razor, shirt, and some underwear. It is our *being* God has loved, and this is why we can accept it. Religion, with its primal verbs in order, is a

continual being born. "When *Thou* is spoken, the speaker has no
thing."[3] It is being who speaks and being weighs as much stripped as
dressed. Our doing and having add no weight. It is *I* that God accepts
and I must therefore love me.

I heard, sometime in the afternoon, that shrewd manipulation
from outside had cost him his lifetime business and several million
dollars. In the early evening I dropped by just to see what, if
anything, I could be. He was sitting in pajamas on his bed, eating a
ripe banana, smoking his perennial pipe, and reading the New
Testament (something about barns, I think he said). I went on
home.

THE CHRISTIAN ESSE

The Christian genius—its incredible view of and unlimited
descriptive-prescriptive ability to talk *to and about man*—rests on the
Christian essence:

Man is what man is because God is in history, our history, as a
Father, looking for children estranged and strayed, as one who cares
utterly. In Jesus the Christ he has done his caring, coming, and
seeking so as to participate in our longing, suffering, and needing in
such a way as to make sense of it. He not only, in Christ Jesus,
demonstrates that our suffering belongs to sense and meaning, but
also he sews up the torn places and anoints the scars. Then he lays
upon us a holy commission.[4]

Our response is an identification,[5] a recognition. We see him in our
own affairs and meetings, our comings and goings. We identify him in
our doings and with him in our becoming. Our answer is thus an
opening up, a willingness for life to flow through us. We become
learners, disciples, hearers, and bearers.

The result is a way, a life, a being-made-whole. It is, as Soren
Kierkegaard described, a courage to be myself before myself and the
Self in whom I am grounded.[6] This life is an open-ended life. It moves
through all the rooms at my house at whatever rental. It is a
receptivity, a royal knowing who I am, a walk toward, a turning from
and to, a relation in awareness, a responsibleness.

And it is a priesthood. I become competent to be the rest of someone. I am a mediating man with an expectancy in which I keep meeting Christ everywhere I go.

Not a possession, it is a being possessed. Not a seizure, it is a being seized. Not a closure of the fist, it is an opening of the hand and heart. Not propositions to which one must assent, it offers relations which one accepts. It is a willingness to be, not an urge to have. And above all, the Christian being is a *hope,* a hope of having not yet arrived.[7] A hope that the last word is not "frustration," that "more to follow" still goes at the end of every page. This hope is the confidence that my obedience and hungry unfilledness, my fears and questings do matter and do participate in a coming and a kingdom that matters. This which we see and say is the temper we had lost from the mortar of our time.

Given our genius (something about *man*) and the essence of faith (something about *being* that ends in persons) in a material-spiritual universe where the risk is always that Spirit may drown in stuff, can you stand a straight look at how we have distorted these insights in the attempt to keep them alive?

How does one keep a great idea? Always and everywhere one answer: he builds a bucket to hold his idea and keep it safe. He makes an *institution*. But then, generally and everywhere, he turns his energies to preserving the *bucket* at great threat of loss to the idea, the content of the vessel.

Look what we Christians have done to the wine by our attempts to keep the wineskin safe. Christian history is the story of what the Word has done to the world; and poignantly, what the world has done to the Word. The Word about Being is mortar that would hold the inhabited world of men together, except that everywhere we have been so anxious to build a house to hold our insight that we threaten to turn the mortar into mud.

How can we begin to come at our true worth-of-being again?

3

THE RECOVERY OF FORM AND SHAPE

Even those of us who see and say this are covered in dismay, just now, because we are caught like Bom and Pim in Sam Beckett's *How It Is*. Mud or mortar, it hardly matters when the mortar is untempered and the tools with which we work are lost or broken. As for that, untempered mortar *is* mud, and the disappearance of the forms and shaping tools means that our genius, our view of man, cannot be put to the shaping of our world without recovery of the temper, frames, and tools—or the discovery of new ones. The church has no real meaning for us in the nominative case unless it has also a dative case. Its meaning as the name of something precious is empty unless it is also a valid means to a worthy end. Our genius must have a house to live in, and this means tools, tempered mortar, forms, and shapes: it means the recovery of symbols or the discovery of new ones. The tension between institution and fellowship, form and spirit is perennial and will not go away. Symbols preserve the life of spirit even in its symbolic house so long as they remain valid symbols. Symbols rise up out of the value they depict and participate in the value itself; we do not invent symbols; they find us. What now is the shape of our situation *vis à vis* the church and the world? How is it with the lamb, the hammer, and the anvil? How is it with the church, its power to shape, and the culture on which, in which, or over against which the work is done?[1]

THE LAMB AND THE HAMMER

Throughout his fifty-three years in that huge and garishly lighted forge, with furnaces, trip-hammers, and drop hammers to heat and pound hot metal into shape, my father never made knives or guns or any weapons—just plows. They were made to cut and tear the rich soil of Georgia, Alabama, South Africa, Australia; they were turning plows, hillside plows, cultivators, gangplows, drag plows for orchards, for cotton and row crops, or for breaking up new ground with deep running points of hard-chilled steel to cut roots. Once I saw one of our plows leaning against a tree on a pineapple farm in Paraguay and wondered if I had hammered it out during some summer work season.

I remember best my father's way of designing new shapes for plows to do new tasks. With a block of tempered mortar (plaster of paris), draw knife, calipers, and his eye he carved a shape, cast the rough metal pattern, and then with hammer and anvil finished his primal form from which millions like it could be made. I recall his battered anvil, still intact, with a half-dozen split and burled hammers, made useless and thrown aside, leaning against the base of the anvil. These are figures as old as Jeremiah's writings and are symbols with which we can work again.

Three times Jeremiah uses "hammer": The Word of God is a hammer "which breaks the rock in pieces" (Jeremiah 23:29, RSV). The "hammer" of the earth "is broken." (See Jeremiah 50:23.) And again, "You [Cyrus?] are my hammer" (Jeremiah 51:20, RSV), the hammer God would use to smash Babylon. It is a good strong literary figure. God had used the Assyrian hammer and thrown it away! Or again, in A.D. 732, Charles Martel (the Hammer) turned back the Muslim armor at Tours and Poitiers, for the salvation of Western Europe from Mohammed.

In the Jeremiah fragment, the persistent metaphor, however, is *sheep.* Israel is a hunted sheep about to be restored to its pasture. The hammer is the weapon God will use against the enemy of the sheep. As a consciousness of covenant takes hold, Yahweh is seen as the kinsman-redeemer who will *do* something. Cyrus is his hammer for smashing stupid and empty forms (idols). He will lead a breakthrough to freemanship.

Centuries later, the church in its medieval splendor thought itself to be God's way of fulfilling God's craft in and upon history. God would use the church as a hammer to make and shape kingdoms for the benefit of his sheep. The Reformation Church, and all Protestantism since, have felt our forms and structures to be tools of the work of God on the world—until lately.

A BATTERED HAMMER

Some have pointed out that the church is in trouble and knows it's in trouble. This is demonstrated by the fact that God is many times more apparent in secular movements, such as the civil rights movement and the fight against poverty and hunger, than he is in the churches. But this is not news. For 150 years some Kierkegaard or Nietzsche or one of the Niebuhrs has been telling us. In particular it is true that this insight did not come upon us with the advent of the space age. Indeed, this insight helped bring the space age about. Atomic energy, modern orbiting devices, etc., are by-products of a new time noted more than sixty years ago (1913) most graciously in a chapter entitled "The Intellectual Temper of the Age," appearing in the volume *Winds of Doctrine* by George Santayana:

> The present age is a critical one and interesting to live in. The civilisation characteristic of Christendom has not disappeared, yet another civilisation has begun to take its place. We still understand the value of religious faith . . . appreciate the pompous arts of our forefathers; we are brought up on academic architecture, sculpture, painting, poetry, and music. We still love monarchy and aristocracy . . . local institutions, class privileges, and the authority of the family. . . . even feel an organic need for all these things, cling to them tenaciously, and dream of rejuvenating them. On the other hand, *the shell of Christendom is broken.*[2]

The "shell of Christendom is broken" (pre-World War I), Santayana says—broken by three hammers: "the unconquerable mind of the

East, the pagan past, [and our] industrial socialist future." These all confront Christendom with their equal authority. Hence,

> Our whole life and mind is saturated with the slow upward filtration of a new spirit—
> *that of an emancipated, atheistic, international democracy.*[3]

The thought of an emancipated, atheistic, international democracy makes every Tory shudder, but it probably carries as it comes "something positive and self-justified, something deeply rooted in our animal nature. . . ." It has its inspiring moments and is "pregnant with a morality all its own." And more, it has possession of us already! The new, as always, has crept up on us from the rear. In the face of it, all around us prelates, bishops, missionaries, and new B. D. seminarians are going back to "honest work" or moving over into social action. The extremes of reaction are "amiable as well as disquieting, liberating as well as barbaric." [4] Some of us are eager for it. We are like Jonah who would rather have seen Nineveh fall than get it saved. Others are as Goethe said of his successive love affairs:

> It is sweet to see the Moon rise while the
> Sun is still mildly shining.

Regardless of our attitude toward the new, since Santayana prophesied, all hell has broken loose to hasten the emergence of a secular age. New movements in theology have purported to face the new secularity with a new Christology.[5] But this will probably not do either; its proponents have no place for mystery and have committed the crime of the abomination of too much of our history. Be that as it may, we do have on our hands a world that does not really believe in God, a secular world with an ethic of shifting utilitarian authorities. The confusion is contained in none of our systems; everything is threatened; and the disturbance is at home in the average individual.

There is a writhing, striving quest on the part of the literate churches to find how to work and live in this new world. God's hammers are at work everywhere that tensions have a part in shaping us. But, as always, the big hammer is the restless, eager spirit of man. "Dynamic change and revolution are to be expected because God is a dynamic being . . . engaged in the active direction of history to his own goals."[6]

What a great stir and buzzing in the world! Just what is coming off here? I do not know and dare not try to say unless it is something such as Abraham Maslow calls our "en-manning;"[7] or such as Dietrich Bonhoeffer hoped for in the phrase, "Man come of age." Most hopefully of all, Pierre Teilhard de Chardin calls it "the divinisation of human activity."[8] Whatever it may be, it's no time to bail out. Come, join in the revolution, for while you can be sure the Christian faith will change, you may also be certain that we shall have somewhat to say. After all, man, the subject we know most about and have most to say about, is at the center of the storm. We have this capacity for talking to and about man for a purpose: to be a hammer of God in the world. Here we ought neither to be trapped nor diverted. We ought not to blunt our hammer at work which others can do better (we really do not need to build a Christian sewer system, while even our efforts to make a Christian educational system are woefully un-Christian and generally poor education). We ought not to get in the way of better hammers God has got; nor are we to beat on one corner of the work until it is misshapen and twisted.

We have our own work: it is to make persons in this world, persons who will make a society fit to live in a kingdom that is coming. The very tools of our trade equip us best of all to hear and call out persons for the work God is doing in the storm.

THE LAMB AND THE ANVIL

God has many hammers at work in the world, but the church is not one of them. Anytime we have tried to play the hammer we have broken our own head, and here we are. The shell of Christendom is broken. This age is not our age to rule. Instead, as Santayana saw, we see an emergent, emancipated, atheistic, international democracy. The big hammer is still the restless eager spirit of man. And the church? We are not a hammer. We are a people whose leader has been traditionally referred to as a Lamb.

If we can liken the church also to a Lamb, it is a healthy Lamb, statistically, but a fifth-rate force in the world. Says Arnold Come in his *Agents of Reconciliation,* "the church finds itself today in the anomalous position of being resurrected in its body but still in search of its spirit."[9] If the German State Church could list 95 percent of German citizens as members, with 5 percent actively concerned, we can do almost as well. The American church is subject to another kind of enslavement. What difference does it make really? Legal establishment as there, or cultural identification as here: they are the same.

The anvil upon which the shape of the American church has been hammered out is our culture, not vice versa. We tried to shape America and were shaped in return. But the force we were able to apply, while considerable, was never as great as we had thought, and was more mystic in character than real. Our ideas about the Christian devotion of the colonists are terribly exaggerated. They really were after something else! Less than 5 percent of colonials in the early eighteenth century had any church connection at all.[10] It is true that certain spiritual ideas had a place, but so did spiritual ideas have a place in Rome, Greece, the Renaissance, and the French Revolution. The *really* effective operational base of American culture *was a kind of nature worship.*[11]

Not until the atomic space age did anything break on Europe to compete with the discovery of the New World in the late fifteenth century. From the early 1500s into the 1800s literature is filled with impossible extravagances of nature in the New World. Especially among Anglo-Saxons, the profound influence of, the dominant place of, and the radical devotion to nature is the development of America from 1640 to 1960. Niagara and the valley of the Genesee, the Ohio valley, the High Plains, the Great Mountains, the Great Lakes, the Southern Pampas and the Mississippi valley, the Great Desert, the West Coast—these were the places for timber, hides, beef, oil, iron, coal, wheat, corn, cotton, silver, and gold. The acquisition of any of these pitted a man against *nature,* and nature was unbounded in her willingness to bless the strong man. This is a great source of our vaunted individualism, which all the frontier denominations made into a dogma; this is the "frontier spirit."

In the main, by the 1880s, the cities where cotton, wool, and silk became fashion, where ore became steel, where cattle were turned into beef and sausage, these were the province of later immigrants, except for a trading-banking constabulary of "older" families, but nearly all were European and all believed in the special qualities of nature in the New World.

Hence, the concepts of nature's bigness, her prodigality (gifts for the taking), were the real shaping of American enterprise. Every American insurance empire rests especially on a worship of nature. It's the way things are here: to plant and to grow— this is nature's way! Our attitudes toward other people and nations in "less fortunate" locations are an extension of this adulation of nature's local expansiveness. Big business is really not so much reflective of a European or Italian banker's model. [12] It is rather a reproduction of nature's scheme of things: you plant, you tend, you water, you work, you wait, and you will *reap!* And nature is still big business, for tourism is especially consonant with nature, even when we go over, through, and under it too fast to take it in. Our past, then, is not so much a mere materialism as it is a *naturalism;* i.e., our creed means: the way of nature is always the way of expansion.

From the 1890s and the time of the earlier Roosevelt, this meant *foreign* expansion. Free land was gone; the widely scattered parts were tied together by ribbons of steel rails; and the new grain land, timberland, irrigated cotton land, and produce land were absorbed along the lines of the rail network. The desperate effort of Republicans to extend their fifty-year dominance past Hoover without free land for nature's expansion would have been the same with any other party in power. The demand was for *expansion.* To this day the company that cannot expand can only merge with one that can expand, or shrivel. And unless we can do better (in 1974) than 6 percent on foreign exports, we are really deep in trouble! The big ideas were nature and expansion. That is to say, *nature's way is the way of expansion.* When land runs out, you trade and ship abroad. You hunt new markets. *The Philippine War was in part fought to lay a base for the China trade!* [13]

What were the effects on American Christianity, the shaping power of the cultural anvil? Incalculable! And notice: where were the big centers of American Protestant mission? China, Brazil, West Africa.

Now read the speeches of McKinley, Cleveland, Roosevelt, and William Jennings Bryan. Where did we wish to trade? Number one was China, which we had to have to make our West Coast, and where we ached to replace Great Britain; then Brazil, where we welcomed the "republicanization" symbolized in the fairly quiet fall from power of the Portuguese "Emperor" Dom Pedro (the best they ever had, so far); then, West Africa, with the Congo basin opening up for ivory and dyes, which we wanted, and timber, *which we did not want,* not even yet!

There had been British missionaries on nearly every boat to India for a hundred years, but the *flag* was that of the East India (Trading) Company.[14] Look: Miss Lottie Moon, the Hudsons, the Inland China Mission, and a hundred others all went to China under the greatest flag of concern to trade with China in our economic history. You tell me what this means. Miss Moon did not know this, nor did I until here of late. She broke her engagement to Crawford Toy (of later Harvard fame, but then at Louisville), convinced he was Unitarian and that she must give her life to God's service in China; and hundreds both preceded and followed, but who can minimize the wave of economic expansion that sent them all serving?

This cultural anvil shaped other matters than missions among the denominations. Nature's way as expansion became God's way in everything of concern to the denominations: evangelism, organization, statistical prowess, stewardship, competition—even in mission. In spite of the throbbing power of the early Moravian "Ye Christian Heralds, Go, Proclaim" and the later "In Christ There Is No East or West," look at the hymns composed between 1890 and the 1920s. Read the "official" and "house-organ" theologies and preachment. Read the "Journals of Work" of the various summer assembly programs from Chautauqua to D. L. Moody's place at Northampton. Also look at the minutes of officialdom, the denominational myths and histories, the path of synodical and local leadership, the new communion with banks and bankers, the financial campaigns of the twenties, the wave of physical expansion, and the proliferation of concern for denominationally oriented sectarian education which saw the birth of at least six hundred small colleges—then let us not talk so much about *Communist* notions of economic determinism! That's only one-half the scope of *that* idea!

"I kicked in my share on the Billy Graham meeting," the banker said to me. "It will bring as much to town as when the Washington Senators opened here last year."

Who is using whom? And what is our driving force?

Against this shaping anvil, that nature's way is the way of proliferation, and after decades of blindness, the church, here and there, has life enough to grope for its proper shape and spirit. (As Arnold Come says, we have our body, but not yet our soul.) This contemporary insight is forcing us into a reconstruction of our legitimate world mission, evangelism, and education, *and* we are discovering, by way of the recovery of the motifs of Old Testament life, a pristinely clear model.

For example, Isaiah 41 is a protest against the cultural anvil that was shaping their gospel, too. The shaping force was, as now, the cultural values of a people, a culture that rested on *their own craft with nature.* The burden of the prophet is (and was) that the meaning and purpose of their community of faith had a different end: Yahweh speaks, "But you, Israel, are my servant, you are different [because] you are mine. You will wear out the anvils of the culture-smiths that would shape you!" (summary of Isaiah 41:8-16).

Now, what about our quest for the church's proper spirit? In this "new" world, what about this new international, atheistic, emancipated democracy that has cracked the shell of Christendom? Against this expansion of the notion of nature's way as expansion, how shall we live in the gospel?

We are being forced to see the preliminary nature of all our life and work behind us. Our gospel began *beyond* us, not behind us. It is incredibly sophisticated in that the gospel *began* beyond our present involvement with nature and craft. We are forced to come to terms with cultures (Canaan) which passed their nature phase and exploited all their resources three thousand years ago! What the gospel is talking about began beyond the worship of Baal (nature and craft) in a world that had already exhausted its reliance on nature's prodigality.

We are being pressed into the discovery of relations that simply have no economic bottom, base, or condition. The crust we have to share is token of an enriched poverty that has no alternative to accepting its 800,000,000 new neighbors. We *have* to get social, if not socialistic, because we have to have our neighbors. We have to care for Asia, Africa, and Latin America because we are in the same world, not because we are rich.

Which is to say, we are forced to give up our reliance on nature's way. It betrays us. Christian ethic begins *beyond* nature worship which empties us, and now we must catch up with our origins after a two thousand-year rondelet.

This means that our only business is the calling into being of persons, all kinds, sorts, and kingdoms of persons. And this changes everything:

preaching, worship, ethics, direction,
education, evangelism, mission,
even stewardship.
(Not many of our job-tasks matter much.)

This problem now means a shift of base. The future is the Christian orientation of adults. If a present generation of adults cannot see this, we have no chance. We haven't the time to show it to the children as our hope. (They have already abandoned what they never had and will catch it only from their pater-familiae.) This means a new schema of adult Christian orientation that can stand to face the myth-systems that have contributed to such a misshaping of the Lamb of God. To this we have now to turn.

THE SHAPING OF THE LAMB

This subtitle, translated as current slogan, means "who is tampering with the soul of the church?" Briefly, we all are. Simon Magus, in the Acts of the Apostles, tried to buy it. (See Acts 8:9f.) It would be to our advantage, too, if we could shape the soul of the church, if we could find it. And God, how we try!

Some of us would trim the lamb with blue ribbons, like a French poodle fresh from the barber, and would have it bleat in Latin.

Some would let the lamb grow wild and wooly on the pampas with no help against briars, coyotes, and wolves.

Some would eat it; some would save it for its wool; some would breed the lamb to death making new sheep. Some would keep it as a toy for kitchen and garden and would show friends passing through just how they love the Lamb.

All of us would like the Lamb of God to be a reflection of our values, ends, and desires. Yet, deeply, we know we cannot really shape the Lamb of God.

I am moved sometimes till my viscera turns over when a sudden revelation from some one of these "I love" shows that they know this too: on the frail side of seventy, bowed under the real power he still has, and moody after the sermon, he stops me at coffee and says, "Is there really forgiveness for a man who hates as I hate?" He knows the Lamb says "seventy times seven." And he can hear me answer "Yes—Yes, since we can talk about it." "Is there reconciliation for an estrangement like ours?" "Would anybody in that lovely place truly love a man like me?" Not everyone, yet, certainly. We know we cannot shape the Lamb, but my God, how we try!

Some weeks a workman sees nothing else but people trying to give their shape to the Lamb:

I left home three hours late in a snowstorm. Having missed three alternative connections, I hired a pickup truck to catch the "Carolina Special" on a siding at Spartanburg in what had become a blizzard. The next day was bright and sunny, but bogged down in deep snow at Lexington and a dozen hours late, I hired one plane, caught another at Louisville, and arrived just in time for dinner before church. It was a charming setting, with sumptuous viands and fingerbowls, in the mahogany-dressed art museum of a private club, and guests. "One" was *big* bonds; two" was big machinery; "three" was a *big* butcher of hogs for the world. The one was a "liberal" with the best wine cellar in the region, I was told; the second was a "fundamentalist" and trustee to a big university; the third was a kind of general Protestant shaper. "Church," I discovered, was to be performed in an old opera house with *box-holders,* no less. After "spirituals" by a visiting Negro choir and

Brahms by an ensemble of joyous professionals, there was "personal testimony" by a *big* oil company executive, entitled for all to enjoy, "The Management Ideal." Then, pièce de résistance! The president of a *big* railroad introduced *me*—to feed the Lamb to a street-level crowd of sinners, seminarians, and Christians before one-quarter of a million TV watchers, it said on the program. Before me, and in me, I guess, there was every jaundiced class ideal, every hung over social pleasure, every cultic crime including a human sacrifice (me) and every agonized need. (Three letters later thanked me for my gospel, and one wanted to borrow some money.)

Reeling out of that one (what a journeyman won't do for hire!), I made a connection, slept the night, and awoke next day in South Georgia. Snow all gone, out the diner window there were wild fields and pine forests, streams with fish and coon-hides hanging on the porches of the little shacks. There were timber, cattle, turpentine, pulpwood, landowners, and sharecroppers.

At midmorning I got up to feed the Lamb again before the volunteered attendance from a state school where nearly one-half of the faculty had (properly) voted to keep me out and the forty-year president had been taught by the forty-year comptroller that I was likely subversive to local interests. My assignment? To mingle three days with some extremely apt and handsome white youngsters who had never in all their lives been thirty miles from home, or twenty minutes into the New Testament, or more than a mile and a half from a Baptist or Methodist church, or within a thousand miles of any issue that mattered to a kingdom that matters.

The most significant action of the week: a sixty-nine-year-old Black hanged himself from a limb so low he could have stood up any second he wished to remain alive in his world of coon-hides, collard greens, fatback, lakes, trees, birds, and sun. His act drew five lines in the local press!

Who is tampering with the soul of the Lamb? We all are! Set over against all this—the Lamb of God. And if I tamper too? I do not know; I do not know. The church that is not so tragic a house would be where we could find together how to look for the Lamb. If I knew, if you let me tell you, it would be a shaping of the Lamb. Congregations (communities) have to find what gospel is together.

Uniformly, in Scripture, in the experience of the early communities, the Lamb is the symbol for what God is doing in the world. He is a symbol of the kind of life-offering acceptable to God. He is descriptive of the character God expects; and he is the symbol of God's victory in the world. Our attempts to shape this mean we wish God to do something else in another way: we wish another kind of offering, character, victory in the world. We want God to enjoy *our* kind of victory. The hammer and the anvil are the tools we use to work on the Lamb, and this is totally incongruous. Lambs are not shod like horses. Nothing one does for lambs requires hammer, anvil, or smithy. The hammer (the tensions that make mankind a seeker) and the anvil (the culture man has lived on), these God will change and bless us with a Lamb; and there is really great difference between helping and blessing. (Most of us can help; many never learn that they could also *bless*.)

This wholeness, this human wholeness, one comes on in Jesus the Crucified, who is the Christ. Proper proclamation has this Lamb and ourselves as subject and subject, but the object is the work of submitting to, receiving, living with this that God is doing. It is the work of the whole community to release the captives, open the eyes of the blind, feed the hungry, care for the bruised, heal the wounds, and deliver them that are bound. (See Isaiah 42:1-8; Luke 4:16-19.) But *only a people who can stand to look critically at their way of life* can see the distortions we have committed on the Lamb. Only such as can submit to the correction of their images of self and society can come into a comprehension of what Frederick Herzog has aptly called *Liberation Theology.*[15]

The only Christian education I know about that would retemper the mortar of our time would force us to look with candor at our value structures. Curriculum headings would appear under every answer candor demands to the open question: *What kind of people are we?* We would have to look at all our folkways, for the pressures that shape the Lamb come from all our centers of concern and value.

The way we serve these is the way we deny the gospel. These are *folkways* and are the subjects with which every history of every society would have to deal.[16] Christian curricula would begin with the answering heads under which we would discuss our real values, by which we would answer "What kind are we?", set over against the best we know of manhood, the Lamb of God.

There is no psycho-*therapy* that does not sooner or later have to know and deal with the sexual fantasies that occupy a mind. Just so— there is no valid Christian education that does not have to know and deal with the myth structures (fantasies) of a society.

Christian education means we have to face our fantasies.

This is where we are. The goal is to put temper, Christian temper, in the mortar. Temper is lime; it heats and stirs, ferments and boils, and turns mud into mortar for a thousand years. This is where we are; and I am frank to say it raises hell in the local parish.

No renewal can come to the church that does not rise in the local parish.

The temper for the mortar is a Christian education of adults that begins where we really are, and would look like this: an exposure of our folkways, and opening of our nerve ends, an understanding of our values, a confession of our fantasies. In all our regions the principal myth systems are these; and this is Christian curriculum, all of which each brings to the confrontation with the Lamb:

The myth about my race, its "purity," its
"superiority," its claim to "divine sanction,"
its "blood and genetic traits," its stereotypes, and the falsities of each. We ask,
from whom am I really descended and in what
species do I participate? How lately were
we cannibals?

The myth about my *class,* its values and treasures,
its bounds of eligibility, its canons of taste,
the real fears that create its "exclusiveness," its
shallowness and falsities, and its short-lived
sustenance.

The myth about my *region,* my own, my native
land, the crassness of my idealisms and
judgments, my false histories and my
fantasies of origin.

The myth about the *nation,* and state and
national interests, the impossibility of
a "national" history, the vanity of our
sources, the falsity of most slogans and
the true nature of a real "patria."

The myth about *economics,* and how all our
systems cover the greed and acquisitiveness
that made jungle survival possible. Work,
property, value, money.

The myth about my *sex,* its strength, superiority,
its permeableness, the difference between
sexualism and sex act. Its perversions as
"answers a smothering child has discovered" (Sartre).

The myth about *family,* including its real
character, the love-hate ambivalence, the
distortions of parenthood, and the tenuous-
ness of relation.

The myth about *religion,* its falsities of
language, claims to superiority, offers of
security, and sources of revelation.

Over against all these stands the Lamb of God, who is not without
witness, by whatever name, in every clime and time.
   Here we could see a rare beginning, threatened with the same end

all "rare beginnings" have had. Some of us are even now able to raise our heads and ask what holds us from the wholeness that seeks us. We are a hope, with others, if we could stand to face the structures we have lived by. For anywhere you meet a whole man, he has at least this: he is able to move in and out of the folkways that surround him. Of course we know—*sociology will not save us!* But critical insight on our systems will convict us and turn us to the Lamb who transcends all our systems—to manhood.

And who has done this? *The* power of the ancient church as reflected in its patristic apologies was just this—they were able to transcend the choking Romanitas,[17] or we would never have heard of them, or the gospel.

> We who formerly delighted in fornication, but now embrace chastity alone; we who formerly used magical arts, dedicate ourselves to the good and unbegotten God; we who valued above all things the acquisition of wealth and possessions, now bring what we have into a common stock, and communicate to every one in need; we who hated and destroyed one another, and on account of their different manners would not live with men of a different tribe, now, since the coming of Christ, live familiarly with them, and pray for our enemies, and endeavour to persuade those who hate us unjustly to live conformably to the good precepts of Christ, to the end that they may become partakers with us of the same joyful hope of a reward from God the ruler of all.[18]

There is a writhing, striving quest on the part of the literate churches to find how to live and work in this world. God's hammers are everywhere tensions have a part in shaping us. As always, the big hammer is the restless, eager spirit of a man. The church, alive in body but not yet in spirit, is not God's hammer, not anymore. It was, instead, victim to the shaping anvil of our culture and the worship of nature expansion. We are forced to come to terms with a faith that arose in cultures that passed *their* nature phase more than three thousand years ago. Our gospel began beyond this Baalism in which we are caught. We are being pressed into the discovery of relations that simply have no race, class, regional, national, economic, familial, or religious bottom. This changes everything we are up to: mission, education, stewardship, preaching, ethic, and worship. This forces us to talk again to, and of, our only concern: Mankind, *men as persons.* This, in turn, raises the central issue of our time. *No renewal can come to the church that does not rise in the local parish.* We have now to see and say what can rise in the local parish with respect to the central issues of the time. It is time someone should tell what can go on inside. It is a hope! If we can face the gravest of the issues that matter, we could stand the rest.

And now, you priest, you only priest there is—how will you come at these contradictions between the shaping culture and the gospel intention, to make us persons? How can we bring our great secret about man to the effective service of the whole society of mankind?

They sit across the table from me in these confrontations: just last month it was *big* insurance, *bigger* banking, *biggest* communications, *brightest* of the law, a *mogul* in textiles, and a real-live educator— utterly faithful churchmen all! And the clichés they threw back at me reflected every expansionistic, nature-worshiping, Baalite, American dream and heretical contradiction of the gospel. Their spoken judgment was that if I had any sense, I'd go along! And to my chagrin I found myself vulnerable even to the fellow who had just missed his chance for priesthood to a veteran employee when she "violated" company mores with alcohol. But what gaps and fissures we have dug between us!

Well, first, in this chapter, we come to see again that we are the only priests God has got. He really does make his appeal in this world by us.

Then, we have to look at the poverty of our appeal and why. It's not our sin—no moralism can do it; it's not our love of wealth, or bloodlines, or wisdom; it's our devotion to our own *false images* of the *self* and *selves*.

And here's the point—I have to get the nerve to submit my me and my false images to the community I trust (my private church) for correction by the highest we know (the Christ)!

And here's the rub: I may lose my life—my special life I've worked thirty years to make.

On the other hand: I may find my life! And indeed, I can count on being met by a very special grace.

And what are these images? Everywhere I have a value I have images: on sex, religion, race, region, economics, family, nation, on and on!

To be an adult means to have finished my tepee. Growth stops and I never have to come out again. But what if my tent poles are less than adequate to support my real personhood?

It's a whole new approach to the Christian orientation-education of adults—without which we have no present chance to be the people we have already said we are.

There's an incalculable grace in it if I have the nerve to submit.

4

THE NERVE TO SUBMIT

For weeks I had been on an exciting and difficult assignment. My work was to confront small groups of navy chaplains with some contemporary challenges, then to respond to their reactions. There were, all told, 120 of us, meeting about eight hours a day, or more; and we were everything: Marines, Nazarenes, Episcopalians, Yankees, Mississippians. We had been to school much and everywhere. We ranked all the way from lieutenant to captain, and every week's session opened with greetings from an admiral! Our graduate and in-service education went all the way up to Menninger Clinic and Harvard Divinity School; we had just about everything, even Ph.D.'s. But everywhere they mostly wanted from me or somebody just one thing.

They wanted the *word,* the *answer,* the *tool,* the gimmick that would establish us in the rank we deserved (whatever the next grade was) as *men* and as *men of God.* To accomplish this, these men had used everything from the Jewish Prayer Book to a bottle of Scotch. They jumped from airplanes, had prayed in Latin, and had slid down forty-foot ropes on their bellies, head first over pools of water. Their citation ribbons looked like cabbage leaves in technicolor, and some even had qualified to wear the Green Beret. But now they wanted the *Word*. And worse, for me, I had been hired to give it.

I remember one especially, a powerful Marine major, who took me by the lapels of my jacket, backed me into a corner and said, "In two weeks I will have three battalions of Marines spread out in the rice paddies of Vietnam and I will be crawling along between kids some of whom have to die and now I aim to hear you say what I can give them. What's the Word for me for them?"

How like an utter fool I felt to keep saying back: "Well, Chaplain, what will you tell them? What *is* your word to men like these?" And that's no answer!

Threatened, doubtful, despairing, aching to be sure of a sure and certain word (which some half dozen were perfectly willing to submit that they had, and wondered why I *didn't),* for days the senior chaplain and I were dumbfounded at the angers exploding, the frustrations gnawing, and the stereotypes being imposed by some of these "finest in the service." Then almost chemically it became clearer. These men were not disgusted with navy duty. They were not frustrated over promotions, or impossible senior officers; these were career men, mostly of senior grade, enjoying the best their rank offered in open opportunity. Rather, the problem lay in quite another direction. It was the same as with the civilian ministry where rank and class are quite as important and even more subtly and powerfully dangerous. And, their angers, while exploding against me, were not truly against me. *These men were frustrated with faith and its terrible silence!*

They wanted God to say something, to say something except those ghastly worn-out words of their creed, or the dreadful alternative of the jazzy *Are You Running with Me, Jesus?* They wanted God to say something. And they wanted a bucket in which to carry it: a form, a Mass, a creed, some dogma, a set of field equipment one could really pack. The Marine major wanted only to be able to deliver.

There's an old story of General Patton in Flanders, turning in a temper to his staff chaplain and saying, "Chaplain, you claim to have divine connections—*stop this damned rain so this army can move!*"

They expected me to *deliver*. And they were desperate enough, threatened enough, to provoke me any way they might force me to deliver what I had been hired to bring. We were all like Elijah, after Carmel. (See I Kings 18:20-45.)

That is, we were like the Elijah to whom God was saying *nothing* there under the juniper. This was not yet *the* Elijah of Koran and all Semitic lore known as the Eternal Wanderer; this was just post-Carmel Elijah, threatened by that woman Jezebel, 180 miles from where his victory at Carmel and Samaria had set her off. The gore of his slaying of Baal's minions still stank in his nostrils and now alone, abandoned and way out of line, he waited for God to *say* something! Anything! In the oratorio *Elijah,* Mendelssohn has him fed here, and the (contralto) Angel sings the utterly moving (and poorly translated):

> "O rest in the Lord, wait patiently for him;
> And He shall give thee thy heart's desire."

(See Psalm 37:4b, 7.)

But either Elijah could not hear, or he did not believe it; or that is not what she sang, for fed, Elijah got up and went three hundred miles farther from Samaria to Sinai, or is it Horeb?

I opt for Sinai, and why would he go to Sinai? There are a hundred high mountains nearer than Sinai. Why Sinai? Simple. He couldn't stand the silence; so he was going where he knew God had been heard from before to see if He would do some more talking. Forty days he went, it says.

And there was an earthquake and a fire and a storm, and God said nothing. (You *must* find and read Barth's almost comic paragraph about who has learned what in these twentieth-century catastrophes.)[1] Elijah listened—quake, fire, storm, and God said *nothing.* Then, to protect us, I suppose, from a truer theology, the earlier translators said that Elijah heard *"a still small voice"!* (1 Kings 19:12, RSV). We Jews all know better. God didn't say anything. "Still small voice" is, in Hebrew, "utter silence." Elijah heard what he was to do next from his own gut response to the silence. He really was, like us, on his own. Ignatius understood it. In his epistle *Ad Trallians,* Ignatius presents the *reality* of the humanity, suffering, and death of Jesus and insists that God has spoken *in the Son.*

THE APPEAL BY US

It's always this way. God is silent, since he has spoken in the Son; and now here the New Testament adds a word we cannot stand and have ignored more than twenty centuries, but it is there! It means *God always has been silent.* Moses *remembered those Ten Commandments;* God did not say them then, either; they were already in other tongues in Egyptian libraries where a king's son like Moses would have studied at school. For example, the Code of Hammurabi, ruler of Babylon around 2,000 B.C., would surely have been in Egyptian libraries of Moses' time. It contains the essentials of our Ten Commandments. He has said all he, God, has ever had to say in the genius of some people or other, more recently and generally Jewish. So, can you stand it? Then hear this exciting, exhilarating word:

He-God-makes-his-appeal-by-us!
He-God-rests-his-case-on-us-and-on-our-character!

Want a text? One of those chaplains I was fighting, an old Lutheran veteran, gave it to me. It goes: "To wit, that God was in Christ, reconciling . . . and hath committed *unto us* the word of reconciliation. Now then, we are ambassadors for Christ, *as though God did beseech you by us . . .*" (2 Corinthians 5:19-20, KJV, italics added). How does God get his stuff across? In what language? He makes his appeal in this world by us.

Perhaps you saw the picture of that impeccably groomed Virginia gentleman, Mr. Raymond Guest, ambassador to Ireland during the John Kennedy administration, on that impeccably groomed gray gelding, accepting first honors at the Dublin Horse Show where as American ambassador to Ireland he was simply trying, he said, "to be the kind of American you would like to have in your country."

How does God get his stuff over?

He was a Negro Air Force sergeant, stripped buck naked by the North Koreans, except for his St. Christopher medal. They let him keep that, says his old cellmate, now a navy captain, so they could taunt him about why his God didn't fix his gangrene! He was still wearing it six months later when he died, stomped to death by "natural causes."

God really does rest his case on us. It's as if a Supreme Court justice accused of high treason should turn his defense over to his young law clerk.

Except that we really aren't beginners anymore. Paul said in his letter to the Corinthians that we are no longer *galaktos* (milk-feeders). We are to be meat eaters now. (See 1 Corinthians 3:2.) We have our long Judeo-Christian memory. We have all our modern insights and discoveries of man and machine and cosmos. We know some biology, genetics, biochemistry, cardiology, endocrinology; some political theory, sociology, depth psychology, and folkways. We have our chance until biology sends something better ashore to taunt us.[2] We have our strength and it is *massive*. We know more and have more to say to, for, with, on account of, and in behalf of man, from here, than from anywhere man can stand. We Christians, I mean. If only we see it, we know a way toward the Ultimate Earth! And that is not a C R E E D; it's a C R E D O!

It's no secret, is it? We never did set out just to build and be a little church somewhere. *We have set out to be the way God makes his appeal and that is more!* It means we have to let the gospel of our real manhood get under the feathers of our protecting images and this is always a *risk*.

THE NERVE TO SUBMIT

I have for years been running into men who are better than their creeds. Creeds kept long make little men. Men who are bigger than their creeds are living a credo, an "I believe," an "I am committed," but the content of commitment is not yet too rigidly spelled out. Credo has to be very careful what it says it believes, and over some words so sacred their meaning is always in doubt, *Credo* stammers. At no single spot does Credo claim that the Mystery is pristinely clear lest it close off new perspectives. Yet, here and there, "I believe" can focus.

If, as we said, God really does make his appeal by us, if he really rests his case on how we do with who we are, if we are the "namers" we are said to be in Genesis (Genesis 2:19), and if we really are the earth's ultimate fulfillment or its continued delay—and—if God's silence waits on our loosing him to speak again by becoming what we have already heard him say we are in Christ—then there is a live question here! *Why God cannot make a better appeal by us becomes important.*

Indeed this would be the whole end and aim of Christian education; to see happen men and women by whom God can afford to appeal! What is this in our way across two thousand years of it? Why cannot God's appeal be better made by us?

Here the genuinely pious always answers: *we are kept from our fullness by our sins,* as if some petty set of moralisms would make us full men! I'm sick of this—

I've known some *real* sinners, by their standards, or mine, whose manhood dwarfs that of many of the pious I have known well; and some of these *real* sinners die pretty good, too.

—the recital of our petty ways of enjoying our state of animal vulnerability. There is a better explanation of our poor appeal than this, or at least a better way to talk about it. In the devotional classic *Creative Brooding* a priest describes his experience of hearing the confessions of the sins of the nuns: "It's like being stoned to death with popcorn."[3] There is a better way to come at the explanation of the poverty of our appeal than by the recital of our petty sins.

And wouldn't we love to escape this responsibility anyhow?

I asked my seven-year-old neighbor how it felt to be seven at last.

"Not so good!"

"Do you wish you were a lot older?"

"No! I would rather be one! 'Cause then I could bite people and they wouldn't bite me back!"

How we love to escape responsibility! How we love to have everything tied down! How we would love to have moral answers that never change, values that never shift, and images that would always hold up! *Then* we could make a better appeal. Fred Speakman first showed me Captain Ahab, in *Moby Dick,* tightening a bench vise on his hand to where he could not move it and wishing profanely that everything in life were as fixed and fastened as his hand. But it never is. Our poor appeal rests on our cursed freedom, or else we could make God's appeal for him with our morality. But the problem lies deeper than any moralism.

Man never faces himself! This is the basis of the poverty of our appeal. We are always evading. Man always evades himself with his images—his false images. *Every culture is held together by its great images.*[4] Here we do have a sure and certain word: false image means false culture just as certainly as false image means false god. "Thou shalt have no other gods before me." "Thou shalt not make unto thyself any graven image." But these two of the ten great ones may not be quite our situation either. Our reading is not deep enough to be true.

In a great book, *Mandate to Humanity,* far too sparsely known, Edwin McNeill Poteat says:

> It has been customary in our times . . . to fulminate against the other gods man has set up before him. Things, we say, or materialism, are man's god. . . . But Wealth is not the god of our materialized, greedy society; it is the altar boy who burns fragrant incense before the grinning Ego god. Or we say Blood is our god . . . [perhaps because] we were born with a good name, or a silver spoon in our mouth, or a pink skin on our body. But social prestige and racism and nationalism are not gods; they too are acolytes before the pedestal on which the ego is perched. Or we say Wisdom is our god. This comes along . . . to flatter the expanding self. Wisdom is gentle and inclined to humility. And God is truth. . . . But Wisdom is no god. It may be an angel hovering about the enthroned ego that strains to catch its enchanted words of praise: "Holy, holy, holy, art thou; the whole earth is full of thy glory." Meaning me![5]

Edwin McNeill Poteat is correct—as he generally is. Our images are ways of worshiping the self. *This* is the poverty of our being appealers for God. We have worshiped the self by fashioning our own *bildung,* as Thomas Mann calls it. We make images and symbols that prove our worth and then fall for the proof we made ourselves.

Against this we have a clear directive. I cited it above: *"Thou shalt not make unto thyself any graven image."* But, says my teacher, Sam, in English this is not a good rendition. It smacks too much of wood carving. Rather read it as it goes:

AL   TA-ASE   LEHA   KOL   PESEL
"You shall not make of yourself a carved substitute
You shall not make an Image of Yourself."[6]

Here it is:

We have made images of the self and believed our images enough to worship them. We have wrapped ourselves in layers of feathers—we have worshiped views of our selves and our surroundings—we have our views of our race, our religion, our economics, our sex, our class, our nation—all our treasures! And now, *hear what I have learned these thirty years:* There *is* no "redemption," and *any claim to "salvation" is a farce, unless it penetrates sooner or later all these treasured feathers of our views of the self—and—this hurts!* This hurts, because our feathers have grown to us. Yet this is the truth I shout from the housetops: *There is no growth that is Christian without the nerve to submit to the correcting of my images of the self.*

I now see it clearly: the spinal cord of redemption is the nerve to submit *all* my images of the self to the Christ and his people for correction. This is Christian fulfillment, Christian growth, and it is superbly the Christian education of adults the hard way; and the Book is clear, if you wish a text:

"If *any* . . .
would come after me
let him deny himself . . ." (Matthew 16:24, RSV).

Let him deny himself what? There's no direct object here. This is always our Christian evasion: we keep trying to put direct objects on verbs that take no object. It is again the difference between *Credo* and *Creed.* William Hersey Davis, in 1940, was denying in his Greek classes that there is any object to the verb "deny." It's just "let *him* deny *himself*"—not deny himself some object! Self is *subject* to be denied; there *is* no object.

I can see it clearer now thirty years later: it means let me have the nerve to submit myself for correction; let me correct my images of myself by the insights of the community. To submit my self-images for correction—this is the church's memory of what God is about, long before there was a social psychology, or Freud's 1911 claim of group neuroses in society; before there was a pseudoscience called sociology, or even Wilhelm Wundt's 1900 version of a *Volkerpsychologie* (Folk-psychology) or the devastating regional psycho-sociology of the South done by the brilliant Howard Odum at North Carolina University, or the revealing analysis of folkways entitled *Folkways* done by William G. Sumner at Yale, or William E. H. Lecky's study of the Middle Ages and social patterns, *History of*

European Morals. The nerve to submit this, my images of me, to the respected other—this is the denial of the *subject,* the self, that issues in clear vision of our human situation.

And where is this correcting to be done? Surely you see through me by now! I am inviting you to free yourself from the dullness of a never ending Sunday school repetition of Zacchaeus, Jesus, and the sycamore tree. I am talking Christian education. I certainly am not saying *sociology is salvation.* I am telling you where we ought to be headed and inviting you to go along. Also I am trying to warn you and soften it, and open it to where we can stand it. *The correction of our images of the self in Christ has to happen among my friends who care about Christ—my real church.* I wish to God I could just say "corrected by the church," but the modern church is the religious institutional encasement of our submission to the images of our society. So, I have to ask you to submit to the judgment of a different church, that small and intimate one, that personal one composed of whatever little group in Christ you are beginning to be able to trust. But the general statement holds: the correction of our images of the self in Christ has to happen in church and the church that can do this for me is church.

Robert McClernon, a brainy and sensitive associate for eight years at Myers Park before he went on to work we judged even more demanding, first preached this submission at our place. I heard it, wept over it, and thought it so high a teaching as to be scarcely heard by the people. But some heard, and I heard the gospel clearer than ever before. There was never a truer reading of Scripture: "*If any will come after, let him have the nerve to submit his images of himself to the community, take up the judgment* [*cross?*] *and come along behind me* [*Christ*]" (Matthew 16:24).

Which set of images can you stand to talk about? Your real church is where you can stand your precious image-values to be talked about.

IF I LOSE MY LIFE

As I was saying, there is no growth without the nerve to submit to the correcting of my images of my-self. The spinal cord of redemption is the nerve to submit all my notions of value and of the self to the

Christ for correction. But that will not stand as is—it's too vague a Christ. *That Christ may look just like the style of life I like best!* The Christ to whom I have to submit my images is the real one: the Christ who appears only "where two or three are gathered . . ." (Matthew 18:20, RSV). This is Christian fulfillment and Christian education. I have invited us to the next level of escape from our exhaustion, the next level of manhood, the transcending of the self through the ventilation of our images we have built.

At once the spinal cord is threatened. If I let anybody go to work on the ideas I live by, something may break! *Exactly so:* there is terrible risk to becoming a new creature. I might lose control. I might get outside myself and be different. I might lose my face.

No! Your gospel has too much risk!

Or as one yet, and still, dear to me, well up on the gray flannel, golf-club-tournament-level, with no guarantees to life missing, a literal modern original of the character in Samuel Becket's play *Waiting for Godot* who says, "Do I look like a man who could be harmed?"—anyway—at breakfast where we were reading the images of Willie Loman in Arthur Miller's *Death of a Salesman*, he hit the table with his fist and pronounced, "By God! I see what it is to be Christian, and I don't really want *any* of it!"

There's just too much risk.

If I look at my *religion*, I might discover how local we are and seek a larger *kathos*, whole, a catholicism.

If I look at my *religious ideas*, I might discover what crutches many of them are and I might have to become a man on my own with only a neighbor to help.

If I should look at my *sex life*, I might have to give somebody room to live—or divorce—or marry—or at least I should have to stop using people as tricks for recreation.

If I should look at my *economic views* with other Christian eyes, I might become guilty, a corporation thief, or see that, as in modern war, I help destroy people I have never seen much less hated. I might even come to disdain money so much that I would turn into a beatnik or a peace marcher. There's a risk!

If I should look at my *nation* through other Christian eyes, I might become a pacifist and embarrass my decorated veteran father by going to prison over refusing military service. It's a risk. And if I should look at *politics* in the light of the four hundred years since Luther, I could not be an American Fascist. If I look at my *race* with the eyes of a Christian community, I might become some kind of half-breed way back there and lose all my lies about my ancestors.

If I look at all my *values* with Christian eyes, they may all melt like a cellophane party dress worn too close to the fireplace, and leave me naked. I might lose *my* life, my special *bildung* I have worked thirty years to make. I would be naked and I might be dead. I could lose *my* life with this kind of gospel. Exactly. There is a threat to the spinal cord of me.

Christianly, I really do have to stop making a graven image of myself. It reads, Jewishly: "Thou shalt not make of thyself a carved substitute for the Eternal One." Translated, it means, "Look out! You will lose *your* life."

Now what is it to lose the life of *me?* What is it to lose *my* life except to give up for correction the notions of what makes my life worthwhile to me? And there's a risk. I *could* lose my images. I *might* lose my standing in politics; I might lose rank in my profession; I might lose my racial purity, my regional pride, my faith, or worse, my job; or I might threaten my family ties. Exactly so. It's a risk. I may lose my life. I may lose every image that holds my me. And, on the other hand: you may already have lost *your* life!

A man may be so dependent upon his boss's good opinion that he becomes a lackey for the boss's wife. He has begun to lose his life.

A man may be so afraid of going contrary to the prevailing winds of opinion in his class or profession that he never opens his mouth and thus opposes the truth. He is losing his life.

A man may be so driven by the goals of his wife that he enslaves himself, unmans himself, desexes himself. He has become a eunuch to satisfy her urge for class and status. He is losing his life.

A man may have such an omnipotence bubble about his own rightness, strength, and competency that he cannot stand any contradiction by subordinates or his family. He has begun to lose his life.

A woman may have such an urge to belong to her image of class or social standing that she will manipulate her husband, children, neighbors, and ancestors to get her fulfillment. She has lost her life back there in her girlhood somewhere.

A man may be so afraid of economic change or loss that he can be pushed all over the hemisphere by an executive whim in his company with no real protest to what this does to his nearest and best loved. He is losing his life.

Wherever you have a set of myths or images about yourself, you can lose your life, your integrity, your manhood. *Your* life is at stake on any of these issues: *sex, race, region, class, vocation, economics, nationalisms,* and *religion.* In any one of these, and add another one, *play,* a man can lose his life.

And, conversely, in any one of these areas, action and being are open to a man in such a way that he can *find* his life. There's a play on words here. Submit your value-images to the Christ where two or three are really gathered! You have nothing to gain but your life. The spinal cord of redemption is the nerve to submit your value images of the self to the highest that the Christian community knows. The man who has begun this has begun to find his life. He has put his *credo* ahead of creed.

I know a denominational executive, worn to the nub by the everydayness of everyday "decisions" about the Lord's real estate. He submitted his images of the self to his son and son-in-law. At fifty-three he is back reading modern theology in a great university, getting ready for any little parish somewhere. He has begun to find his own life again.

I know the former head of a big business, "promoted" out for his public stand on racial justice, who corrected his images of his own future by the church in his own house, returned to the city he had served, job or no job. He has found his life again.

I know a once prominent pastor who submitted his prejudice for correction by his daughter. It cost his job, his lovely home, his thirty-year place in his denomination, and a move of three thousand miles for him to act out his real values. He has begun to live, I hear, running a walk-in laundry with a young black partner.

A young chemical engineer accused himself brutally to his pastor of wanting both to go and not to go at his company's beck and call. He decided what he *really* loves, refused his third and last promotion. "No more being shoved," he said. "I have found my life."

I know the pastor of a great church, they said, who went to Selma because his wife had been unable to keep from going. It cost him old friends and all his golf partners, they said. But he has his life. Another I have loved and wished most to be like, they tell me, had thirty deacons who would not meet his eye after thirty years of a magnificent pastorate that graced a once great city. He had found his life long before. And time would fail me to talk about a pipelayer in Bay City, a chemist in Houston, a pastor in Beaumont, and an IBM supervisor working as a secretary in Brazil. They are finding their lives.

What an incredible source this is from which we take our lives. It keeps talking of a manhood that puts every creed we have under judgment. What do you do with a Book like ours, for example—so open that it lists a seduced seducer, a harlot, and an adulteress, in the genealogy of the Lord himself? (See Matthew 1:1-16). With Tamar, Rahab, and Bathsheba in his lineage what *could* he say about his own ancestral images? What about that! We live, says Krister Stendahl, on 5 percent of our biblical resources—just a way beyond the Golden Rule. But our Lord puts *everything* under judgment and says *therefore choose life.*

It requires much nerve to choose one's life—to jump over the hedges of one's images. Nothing requires more nerve than to put one's feather systems under the fire. Romain Rolland has said, "Dare to detach yourself from the herd."[7] Over against an "oceanic feeling" one must achieve his personhood by standing out from the herd. The Book knew, centuries before Lecky's old study of European morals or Eric Berne's *Games People Play,* that society is a set of games we play, games played with various faces, personages, masks. The Book also shows how the game is upset when any man (Zacchaeus, Matthew) obeys his inner call. All our games are bothered when the person comes out from under the feathers of his personage. "If I lose my life" becomes, here, an "I *must* lose my life," for whoever saves his own life does lose it; it simply never opens. This is perhaps why Soren Kierkegaard preferred to say "choose oneself" instead of the Socratic "know thyself." For choosing here means I have renounced the provincial life of me. I have refused my feathers as my real or my best. I have discovered that to be *person* is the same as to be free.

In one of his early studies, Luther translated "Ye shall know the truth and the truth shall make you free" with the same word he had used for "untying " the ass's foal that Jesus would ride down David Street. This is the goal of our Christian years of Christian community in Christian education: *to untie the man Christ Jesus freed.* There's a play on words here. If I lose my images, I may find my life. It's what the gospel is about.

GRACE AS SHARED ENDURANCE

If God is silent because he rests his case on our character as followers of the Son, if we have been called out to be the way God makes his appeal, if the poverty of our appeal is due to the way we protect ourselves with our self-images (if we really have made idols of ourselves), if there is no changing this without the nerve to submit our images of the self for correction, and if this happens where church is truly church; if the spinal cord of redemption really requires me to submit my self-images to my private church for ventilation of my feathers, you are right who say this is a terrible risk. I may lose my life. Exactly.

She was right when she came to me at coffee hour and said it was cold and rainy out there without her girlhood images and idealisms to protect her. And just maybe he was right the next day at the wedding reception when he said I had fallen off into a different kind of absolute—no compromise on the denial of the images of the self, as the nerve to submit.

Listen! I have wasted half my ministry away from home talking my gospel to people who are kept from hearing me by the stereotypes they have made that I cannot fix. And I've spent half my life at home saying again to people what they did not hear me say. The other halves I've wasted shrilling that all our national, religious, and cultural *ecumenisms* are too small—that Jew, Catholic, Protestant, and Muslim are all children of the same insight; and this idea came from an Asiatic yellow memory far behind that first Abraham. I sum up the whole of my wasted years in a restricted religious group from which I long ago withdrew, for we were not of a kind, by saying: "The only relief from our poor appeal is a proper worship that does not turn *credo* (I believe) into *creed* (the thing believed)." The subject of my believing, the subject believed upon, the Christ himself, has to be free to grow, or change, or be understood. We Protestants are always nailing down insights never meant for nails. Poor Jesus! And poor Luther, too, since the Marburg Colloquy;[8] poor anybody who ever tries to live *credo* without too much *creed!*

So: no absolute. I am a witness, not a creed writer. No absolutes. If you hear me saying ineffectiveness is cured only by your death, if you hear me say you absolutely lose the life of you to be in Christ, I cannot now say so. If you hear this, it is because there is still so much of moralism in our atmosphere. What I lose is the life that is the product of my own image building. What I get back is the *me* that is created for immortality.

At this point, at my first writing, my telephone rang—Western Union—telegram—"Joe M. Evans died today. Funeral at El Paso." Before I could send my own answer, I had been stricken myself from sending messages anywhere, but had I been conscious and able, I would have answered: *He should have lived forever!*

I never knew more man in a little piece. And I never saw him as anyone but himself. I'd bet he had his boots on, or they were nearby with the socks draped over the tops to dry. I know about memories of six hundred bear hunts and thousands of campfires and thirteen thousand head of white-faced Herefords dead of starvation in a single drought in the Davis Mountains of west Texas, and twenty-five years of back-breaking labor to repay every investor. But I never heard of a day he did not submit to the Christ and his brothers his notions of the self for correction. He lived seventy of his years a hundred miles from a railroad and he knew only two books, really: The King James Version and the Texas Almanac. He deserved to stay Joe Evans forever! But only because you could always see *through* him. There was *no* guile, and if you looked, there had been a Jesus around. Why this opening up is so threatening I do not yet know.

"Where is the strength to come from, or the nerve?" she asked after the service. "To be able to submit to such a stripping of one's possessions and protections and values—it leaves me frightened, threatened, chilled." She pushed on, "Is there no *grace* in this situation?"

And before I could say my answer next Sunday, I was learning the facts of Loren Eiseley's claim that *all* life begins and ends with a gasp for air through a snout.[9] But of course she is right. Is there no grace? Indeed! Without the grace who could stand any of it?

What one risks, all one risks, is the fear there will be no grace to catch him if he lets go, no balm for his wounds, no warmth for his chill. He risks the *gracious hearing;* it might not be there! Unless, and yet, does he not have some premonition in advance?

It's six years now since she asked it, but I remember that Sunday morning dawn when out my hospital window the first uncompromising yellows and reds of sunrise were showing across a ridge in the Piedmont and I had a premonition! That big bright yellow round thing was going to come up again. I went on with a second cup of hot tea. I was *sure* the day had come at last.

It is so with grace. Do I not have some premonition in advance that the day will come with grace? I nudge my way into this early dark; I ease my way into this cold water. *I disclose only where and as I am being heard.* (For months it was only Elizabeth or Bob McClernon.) Grace precedes me and calls me out. Don't be afraid! You won't risk a premature disclosure. Grace has already met you before the actual leap. You submit your various images for correction only *where* and *as* grace meets you; and you may discover as you go what some pagan bartender or mechanic has been telling you all along.

Once more: You may discover that what you receive is not censure, rebuke, pain, or a chilled immersion in a baptism that bears the threat of death. You may come upon a great gladness at your coming open. (She had said, "It's cold out there, who can stand this kind of exposure?") And I say, look for the glad rejoicing of learning how to be guilty, too.

At least that was the net worth of the discovery of the other one that last week who ran the risk of telling me: she discovered that when one submits the images to the brother in Christ it may result in a freedom to do *less,* not more. It may give me a freedom to concentrate, not take on more. It may be even a freedom to be guilty and it *will,* I promise, teach you that you really do not have to be a blessing, a successful blessing. *God happens between you!* But that is where I began, years ago, with that lovely person asking me what I thought I could do for her and me muttering like a bashful schoolboy, "Nothing, I reckon." We've gone some kind of circle, but here we are: God happens between you; all you have to be is who you are. And it's all right if the piece of zwieback the baby dropped has dirt on it. Let him go on and eat it. To accept grace is *first* of all to be able to accept my guilt. It's not I who is God's spotless lamb!

The way people I love keep mishearing me is enough to make a man quit preaching, and I have, some say. She actually heard me say that the nerve to submit one's images of the self to the Christ community meant that she had to go back to an old vow made when she was thirteen years old. That vow would require her to leave her husband and children, place and time, to tell Bible stories up the banks of some Louisiana bayou as she had said she would twenty years before! This took nerve! To tell her husband, and timidly to tell me, to submit her images to the church between her best loved and me? This took nerve!

For her, as for me, the gospel has meant the release of a captive, not the binding of a prisoner! For her it meant release from a foolishly specific promise. (A thirteen-year-old child can give herself to God, but not to a Louisiana bayou or even to China, if she lives in Indiana. Of the bayou or of China she can but dream, not promise.) For her, losing her life has meant release from an old guilt, from an old and ungodly rigidity imposed by persons who had no right to extract such a promise but knew no better. Do you hear? Sometimes the nerve to submit results in grace, release, forgiveness, acceptance, confirmation. Not rigid behavioral absolutes, but a grace, a very grand grace. The correction of your moral images doesn't mean a *beating:* it means a new freedom to be. The result of submitting one's images, old promises, and standards is a releasing grace, not a lashing.

And how is this grace demonstrated? In a shared endurance of things, *he takes up his abode in us.* (See John 14:23.) We become one-with-Christ. (This is the union-with-Christ that Walter Rauschenbusch loved in A. H. Strong whose rigid theology he otherwise found so distasteful.) Christ takes up his abode in us; we take our character of openness from him. And for some it means participation in all that Christ is for in the world. For some it means they have seen the Son of Man coming in his kingdom without tasting death; and for some it means that at the little door where all human life is a snout reaching for air through an ooze you neither ask, nor beg, nor bargain, nor pray, you just wait—and *rejoice* at the mileage and relation you have had.

Actually, this shared endurance is the only true catholic and holy church. All the rest are attempts to represent it. For *this* church is a laboratory of maturity in which, by the presence of Christ in his people, the will to hide is broken and the will to will what God wills is given.[10]

And what does God will? Here a thousand brands of presumption are available, for any man who talks the will of God is presumptuous. I choose Paul Lehmann's brand here: God wills "the power to be and stay human . . . to make and keep humanity human."[11] That is, all God wants or needs from us is our coming to wholeness or maturity.

Maturity? It is "the full development in a human being of the power to be truly and fully himself in being related to others who also have the power to be truly and fully themselves."[12] The Christian church then becomes simply what God has done, does, and will do in Christ to make and keep us human. The Insider is the one who has come open to this. The Outsider, whether in or out, no matter how "secular" or "of this age" he may be, is the one who has remained hidden.

At any rate, no one is exhausted in the open! He has a communion, and wherever his endurance of humanity is truly shared, he is in the church and here a very great grace spills over on us all, God's response to our nerve to submit.

"Your proposal is audacious! If indeed we put all our values and images up for correction—sex, race, region, religion, economics, politics, national loyalty—such a storm, such stress, such conflict and tension!"

Precisely.

The community of priests in conflict is not the church failing—or falling apart. The church, with its priests, in tension with its culture is the church in its natural habitat. We ought not to want the kind of peace most of us have craved. It is a betrayal to try to be rid of the torque which heats us to holy dissatisfaction. There is "no hiding-place down here" where the church and her priests share the tensions or lose her Lord.

And who were those who first led us into storm? Apostles? They were lay people, priests, women, and men like ourselves who had submitted their images, just as now. Advance is through storm.

5

CONFLICT AND TENSION

The natives of Tahiti put into their fishing waters an intoxicating mixture prepared from the huteo nut or the hora plant. The fish, drunk with the stuff, float helplessly on the surface and are caught as the fisherman wills!

The average churchman, unworried about the missing consecration that should be the inevitable concomitant of redemption; growing more respectable and less redemptive year by year; serene in the company of other hundreds who have favored God with their presence; dropping his coin as lightly as possible into the hastily passed plate; muttering at the length of the prayers, the quality of the sermon, and the unfamiliar cadence of a new hymn, is a fish of another sort—but just as intoxicated. He is not a *church-man;* he is not a *Christ-ian;* he is a member of a cult. God has far more in mind for his people. A man has to wake up to the tensions around him. The life of the church is always in an atmosphere of tension—wakefulness. Priests are *a part of the surrounding tension.*

Tension is written into all that lives. It is everywhere. "In the tension of the opposites is the mainspring of the Cosmos."[1] Nothing that lives can remain in repose. Nature herself is "everlastingly and furiously dynamic, permitting nothing throughout her whole circumference to be at rest. . . ." [2] The universe is "undeniably at war with herself." [3] The tension is everywhere, even in God, for "to deny tragedy in the Divine life is only possible at the cost of denying Christ, His cross and crucifixion, the sacrifice of the Son of God." [4]

There can be no moral life without tension. The words of tension: choice, distinction, freedom in evil, free will, all mean that moral life is shot through with tension. "The longing for God in the human heart," says Berdyaev, "springs from the fact that we cannot bear to be faced forever with the distinction between good and evil and the bitterness of choice." [5] All moral life is a part of the tragedy and drama of choice.

Life itself does not indicate at any time in any age that the world is on the way to become what it has never been, "a home of rest for the gentle and timid, a sequestered garden for those who hate the turmoil of the sea. . . ." "Life," writes Dixon, "is a perilous adventure, and a perilous adventure for men and nations it will, I fear and believe, remain." [6]

Science and philosophy cannot help us. "They have taken from us our personality, our freedom, our souls, our very selves. They have, however, left us our sorrows." [7] I suffer; therefore I am! I am in tension; therefore I am alive. Everywhere the spirit lives it is drawn taut—for,

> Fate is a sea without shore, and the soul a
> rock that abides,
> But her ears are vexed with the roar, and her
> face with the foam of the tides. [8]

The Christian believes God is in this universal tension. He is in history as its master. The earliest Christian view of history was that God had initiated the historical process by a uniquely creative act; he had supervised its unfolding throughout the years; and he would presently bring it to a close by instituting judgment and establishing a New Age. Until the consummation there is tension.

What if this is true? What if things are as God intended? What if things are just as they will always be? What if there is no hope of a better and easier day? What if there is no automatic progress? What if this tumultuous time is written in, innate, native to humanity? What if God is master of history and history is as he meant it to be? What if you and I are such creatures as can find our God only when beset on every hand? Suppose our minds can find order only in chaos. Suppose this evil order must continue. What if this blind path leads to God? What if we have been slinking aside from the path of tension like sick and perishing animals, seeking a surcease that was not meant to be there?[9]

What if there is purpose in chaos? What if righteousness and morality grow best in man when he must fight against unrighteousness and immorality? What if our message is true?

In one of the great pictures in the Apocalypse the strong angel asked for the opener of the scroll that would reveal the meaning of history. None in heaven or earth could open it, and the confused world remained unexplained. "I wept much," says the writer, but one of the elders said, "Do not weep." And then he pointed to the "Lion of the tribe of Judah." The writer saw no lion—only a Lamb, "as one having been slain," but nearer to the throne of God than anything else. In the light from the seven eyes of the Lamb, the elders and the host understood the meaning of the scroll, and they sang a new song for all tribes and peoples. Their song was about the heart and method of history—a redemptive history. "The redeemed reign on earth," they sang. (See Revelation 5.) And where, in this time of confusion, do the redeemed reign on earth?

The redeemed reign anywhere God uses the tension to effect redemption! In all the turnings of history, God's history has moved toward redemption. The redeemed have been involved in all the turnings of history. Redemptive meaning appears in all the clashes of history. God in history creates history's tensions so that it may move forward redemptively. The line of redemption stays taut.

I heard a seasoned leader of churches, a sociologist who should have known better, dismiss the lifework of Pitirim Sorokin, Chairman of the Department of Sociology, Harvard University, with a deprecatory wave of his hand. One cannot get rid of him so easily; for, when Sorokin says *all life* must go through the tensions of *crisis— ordeal* to reach *catharsis—grace,* to know the release of *new life,* he is using existential terms.[10] All life, even God, is in tension. It is only out of tension that redemption can come.

Let us not make a mistake: *The church, with its priests, in tension is not the church failing. The church in tension is the church in its natural habitat.* The business of the church keeps it always on duty on the borderline of tension between the mighty opposites. The church must always proclaim its resounding "Yes" to a chorus of defiant "No's." But actually the tension is not between the holy church and the secular world. We have kept our sights too low. The church is not the pole of tension except as it is Christ, for Christ is the antipode of world. It is Christ–world, light–dark, love–hate, that form the tensions of the age. The church gets its tensions from its Christ.

I have come to see the tautness within my own ministry, the tension in the churches I serve, the fact that we have never been thus far able to let half-done alone, as the reflection of Christ's pull on us. He exerts his tension on nothing that is dead and incapable of responding. We ought not to want the kind of peace many of us have craved. It is a sin to try to quench the flame of the Spirit that heats us to a holy dissatisfaction. There is "no hiding place down here"; the church must share the tensions or it cannot share its Lord. The church at rest is the church dead. The peace of the church is the suspension of its Lordship in Christ. Whatever peace He promised us, it was not the peace of suspended tension that is death. His peace that passes understanding is not the peace of an amiable indifference, whatever it is. It is God's own peace that can come to us only with the sharing of God's own tensions.

The continuousness of the cross, in the church, is just this tension between Christ–world, light–dark, life–death. The cross in the church means what it meant on Calvary: *something was being pulled apart!*

There is no advance without storm. The church has no business looking for a quiet street, a backwash from life's main currents. It belongs at the crossroads, on the frontiers of human tension. The confrontation of Christ which the church offers is always a situation of tension. The church has no business confronting men with anything save Christ, at any place save the areas of tension. It is by dodging these areas of tension that the church learns to live without

Christ, which means that it is no longer the church. The desire for a tensionless existence is not valid. Cessation of tension is certain death. What is desired is victory, which, by a strange paradox, is *already* won! It is only "the great Church victorious" that "shall be the Church at rest."

What are the points at which the church is always in a state of tension with the world? What are the areas within which this gospel-world tension always appears?

Between the years A.D. 50–100, says Harnack, there began to appear

communities who believed in a heavenly Church, whose earthly image they were, endeavoured to give it expression with the simplest means, and lived in the future as strangers and pilgrims on the earth, hastening to meet the Kingdom of whose existence they had the surest guarantee.[11]

What were the areas of tension, conflict, and cross between these communities and their world? Through what storms did the church advance in Acts? Which of these tensions are common to the life of the church in all ages?

If the church is Christ as he continues to appear, redeem, and call, then the tension will be felt at certain points of contact. That is to say, if the church confronts the world with a Christ who is appearing, redeeming, and calling, and this confrontation results in conflict-tension, it is because there are other and rival appearings, redeemings, and callings.

The tension of the church will appear in all ages like this:

Church	*World*
Christ-appearing . . . confronts . . . world-appearances	
Christ-redeeming . . . confronts . . . world-redemptions	
Christ-calling . . . confronts . . . world-callings	

It is tension, conflict and advance through the storm of rival claims: a conflict of *gods,* a tension between *values,* a pulling apart of *vocations.*

Everywhere the church advances, it will be against other reference points for worship, other redemptions, and other callings. If this is valid for all ages, it will appear from the first in Acts, as well. We may then expect to find the church struggling with other *gods,* other *sets of values,* and other *callings.* Is it so in Acts?

In Acts a number of rival reference points for worship appear. The church meets them head-on, in a state of tension from the very onset.

The first encounter was with temple worship and the "Law of the Jews." When Peter lifted the lame man at the Gate Beautiful (Acts 3:1-6); in his addresses before the High Priest's party and before the court; during his imprisonments; in his going to the Gentiles (Acts 3, 4, and 5); in the furor over circumcision and the keeping of ceremonial law (Acts 10:9-48); in all the journeys of Paul, at Derbe, Lystra, Iconium, and especially in the Jerusalem-Caesarea sequence, the great conflict is with the claim of the temple on the hearts of all Jewry and the power of the Law to control their lives and worship (Acts 13–26). Paul's circumcision of Timothy is a concession to the Law (Acts 16:1-4); one agony of his ministry was out of the tension of Spirit versus Law, church versus temple, as it appeared *within* the church by way of the Judaizing elements (Acts 24:1-9). He had not transcended one ghetto to build another!

Everywhere the church has ever gone, it has had to deal with rival temples and rival sets of Law. Consider demon worship and spiritualism, magic, and necromancy, as they first appeared in the conflict with Simon Magus in Samaria, in the "certain magician" of Acts 13:6, the witch doctor on Cyprus (Acts 13:6-12), and the "magicians" of Ephesus (Acts 19:19). Notice the ancient and competing God-appearances of the time. The characteristics of Zeus and Hermes are found in the people at Lystra (Acts 14:8-18). The men of Athens, the city of idols, thought Paul mentioned two new gods when he spoke of Jesus and the resurrection, and they tried to laugh him out of court (Acts 17:30-32). Artemis, goddess of the Ephesians, combination Great-Mother and harlot, could prompt an uproar hours long at the pressure from the gospel of Christ (Acts 19:29-41).

The genius of Rome, shrine of worship for sixty million people, later caused the martyrdom of thousands as it struck back at young Christianity. Rome, the reference point for worship, was the enemy and antipode of the church at Philippi, colony of Rome. The opposition of the "city authorities" at Thessalonica (Acts 17:5-9), the charges against Paul that in Jerusalem he had spoken against "Caesar" (Acts 17:7), were but further examples of the tension between theophanies. For that matter, the name "Caesar" never appeared without the accompanying thought of worship of the empire. Caesar was more of a religious term than a political one in the world the church in Acts was facing.[12]

Anywhere the church advances, it is through the storm raised by lesser gods in tension with the God of the church. Paganism has never been synonymous with atheism. All men have gods—*Der Mensch habt Gott oder ab-gott,* "The Man has God or an idol," Luther said, and the ages attest it. It is a principle that will hold. There is no tension within the particular church, nor within "the whole church," that is not there in part because of some loyalty to some lesser god. Whether the god be Mammon, Mars, Demos, Astarte, or some other, the world has still to know the so-called *Gotter-damerung,* the "twilight of the gods." It has never been twilight for old gods. They do not die. In our day there is a great renascence of the gods. The church must meet them, every one, even where the god is myself, with its confronting Christ; and this brings tension. The advance is always through the storm raised by the resentment of lesser gods. How painful, how fraught with tension, is that historical process whereby an old world finds a new God and judges its old ones worthless![13] Anywhere Christ appears, there is the confrontation with lesser gods, lesser appearances.

Wherever the church is Christ-redeeming, wherever the continuing cross-deed is known, it confronts *other* "redemptions," other sets of values, other estimates of worthwhileness.

In Acts 4, the church runs counter to the great value system of tradition, the way of our elders. That is to say, in Acts 4, the church was a Troeltschean sect,[14] refusing the *paradosis,* shaping tradition, of its elders. Young modern free churches face the same tensions. The references throughout early Acts to the high-priestly family, the Herodians, the people of Israel, the Sanhedrin, the Pharisees, and the Sadducees, are references to competing schemes of value held by men who found themselves in tension with the larger redemption.

The conflict of Stephen with the Society of Freedmen, the

Cyrenians, the Alexandrians, and those of Cilicia and Asia was an expression of the tension that arises when Christ-redeeming confronts lesser redemptions of earth. In the preaching of Stephen, the larger redemption literally forced open the bonds of Jewish exclusivism. The temple was not exclusively holy, for wherever God is, there is the temple. Israel had always resisted God's mercy; they were the real lawbreakers. In the ensuing explosion of pent-up tension, Stephen was smashed to death, but exclusivism died, too, in the thrust and pull of the Christ-redemption.

The first encounter of the church with ethnic barriers, provincialisms, and especially Jewish-Gentile distinctions was the confrontation of the larger frame of redemption with the narrow cellisms of a lesser scheme of value. The Christ-redemption melted the barriers everywhere; it brought about Christian relationships between Hellenist and Hebrew widows, with an Ethiopian, with a Roman, with the Greeks at Antioch, and with other Gentiles. From the time of Pentecost the tension is apparent, with the larger redemption always prevailing. This is the point of Acts: the freeing from old tyrannies. It *is* a *Liberation Theology* (Frederick Herzog).

The provincialisms of Pharisaism, Alexandrian semi-Christianity, Athenian sophistication, and Ephesian patriotism died out here and there before the claim of the *larger redemption*. This happened in Paul's own experience. It happened to Apollos through Priscilla and Aquilla (Acts 18:26). By Paul's hand it happened in Athens (where two, at least, believed) (Acts 17:34) and in Ephesus (Acts 19). Even Epicurean evasion and Stoic disclaimer came in for a jolt from the hammer of universal redemption (Acts 18:4).

The redemption of materialism, also, was strong enough to create a tension and was credited for the death of Ananias and Sapphira (Acts 5:1-10). Later, the tension between Christ-redeeming and the prospect of money-bought redemption caused Peter to say in strong words to Simon Magus, "To hell with you and your money!" (paraphrase of Acts 8:20). The result of the first was an outbreak of healing on the wings of the great redemption. The second brought the release of the gospel in Samaria.

Anywhere the church advances, it is through the storm raised by lesser redemptions in tension with Christ-redeeming in the church. It is a principle that holds. There is no tension within your particular church or within "the whole church" that is not there because of the claim of some lesser redemption. Whether it be the redemption offered by tradition, racism, sectionalism, or materialism, the church advances by meeting and surpassing in redemption.

The church is Christ-calling confronting other callings, others on a mission, other destinies, from the beginning.

Again and again His imperative call has harried men out of the rabbit warren of their own desires to go serving him along some dusty road. When the church is actually Christ-calling, Christ's imperative call is still no less urgent. Anywhere the church advances, it is through the storm of lesser callings that exist in tension with the great call, the greater destiny of God in Christ in man. It is an axiom: *Anywhere the church redeems, it makes a new redeemer.*

The book of Acts is permeated with this tension. Almost everywhere it gives a name, it gives the calling of the named. Around twenty different callings, ways of life, are mentioned. In more than one calling the tension from the lesser call is winner, as in the cases of Felix, Festus, and Agrippa, but the call and the tension can be felt everywhere in Acts. The book is really about lay-priests from everywhere, and this is the point of all the references. All are priest and all are lay.

Among those whose calling was to empire, to government and power, to Caesar and the genius of Rome, or to some lesser Rome, there were Manaen, a member of the court of Herod; the Ethiopian, treasurer for Candace; Felix, the governor; Festus, the governor; Agrippa, the king by grant; and Sergius Paulus, the proconsul.

Out of those whose calling was to trade and service, came Lydia, the merchant; Simon, the tanner; Barnabas, the landowner; Rhoda, the serving maid; Dorcas, the seamstress; Aquila and Priscilla and Saul, tentmakers; a slave girl in Philippi; and even Demetrius, the silversmith, dual slave of Artemis and his trade, was called.

Among those whose calling was law in the sense of order and control, the greater call cut across to Cornelius, the centurion; the Philippian jailer; the centurion and the captain on a sailing vessel; the host, Publius, on the little island of Malta; Gamaliel, the teacher of the Law; and Crispus, ruler of the synagogue at Thessalonica.

In steady procession through Acts they come: Barnabas, Silas, Mark, Timothy, Demas, Luke, Titus, Apollos, and lesser names.

Who are they in Acts? They are men of any calling who will hear the higher calling to become redeemers themselves! They are men who will submerge the lesser in the greater, men who will assume the agony of the following, *men who will redeem as they were redeemed; men of the universal priesthood of believers, without benefit of clergy, rank, ordination, education, or position;* sharing only one thing, the redemption of our Lord Jesus in the church in God.

Anywhere the church advances, it is by a countermarch across the fields claimed by lesser callings. Anywhere the church exists, it is vocation, never avocation. By the call, the church preserves its redeeming witness in the creation of other redeemers. It is always in tension that the call reaches the called one. It says "come out from among them"—and "them" is always the lesser call.

The world has always had its called ones sent on its own limited missions of limited redemption. All men know some lesser calling. There is no tension within your particular church or in you that is not there in part because of some lesser calling. Even the calling and destiny of inertia, mediocrity, laziness, and comfort have their tensions and their claims. Every victory for the church, each advance, represents the submergence of some lesser calling in order that the redeemed ones may become redemptive.

Indeed, the advance is through storm. It is the storm that is raised by the tension between Christ and lesser gods, between the Redeemer and lesser redemptions, between the Calling and lesser callings. Anywhere the church advances, it is by virtue of victorious tension exerted over and across the claims of lesser gods, limited redemptions, and lower callings. The church has no other enemies with whom it could be in tension, for even Satan is but a lesser god.

The "advance through storm"[15] both required and produced a new race of men. Their tools and the constant demand for adjustment, their powers of accommodation, and their developing forms require a wider backdrop than the book of Acts. But the story of advance is without real point unless we return to the point where tension began, within the lone priest man looking for the victory.

What is the application of the advance by storm, of the life by tension, to the single Christian man? What does this mean to the man with whom we began, half awake, stirring, only beginning to become, but arrested in the process of becoming by the lethargy around him, yet uncomfortable in the conviction that something lies beyond the horizon in Christ that he has not yet seen? What does it mean to him? Is there no surcease from tension for him?

The ultimate application of the tension is within each man. There is no meaning in the conflict with lesser gods, lesser redemptions, and lesser callings that does not come as the result of the same tensions in individual souls. The "advance through storm" by the church is after all an advance through storm by the lone Christ-man, too.

And there is no surcease apparent in the tensions even here. From the height of eighty years came the insight that prompted a handwritten last line appended to a letter from my teacher, Dr. William Owen Carver. He had wished me Godspeed in my own pilgrimage of the Spirit in the body of that prized letter, then, after it was typed, had written in the prayer that my travail might be the means of God's setting some feet *"on the restless and ofttimes stormy road to peace."* After eighty years of tension is it then still a restless and ofttimes stormy road? Of course it is. For Christ stands within the tension confronting the believer with always newer heights of His appearing, redeeming, calling.

If there is tension within the particular church, it is but the sum total of the tension within its stirring, searching lay-priests. There is no advance through storm for the church except as there is advance through storm for believer-priests who have become redemptive through a measure of victory over lesser gods, redemptions, and callings.

The tension between Christ-world is the same as the tension between church-world, as is the believer-world tension, too. The cross in the church, the cross on Calvary, and the cross in the believer are of one and the same meaning: something is being pulled apart.

There is no advance without storm for the believer, for he has no more business on life's quiet streets than the church has. He belongs on the frontiers and at the crossroads of human tension. It is by dodging these areas of tension, by avoiding the pangs of advance, that both church and believer learn to be something other than Christ. The desire for a peaceful existence is not valid. Cessation of the conflict is death in the believer, too. The advance is always by the storm of tension created in the conflict with his own little gods, his own little redemptions, and his own little callings.

There is no surcease with honor or with life. There is always something about the mountain that says man has to climb it; and in his climbing, Christ advances, by storm. But there is no place where the lone believer stops. Even his consummation is further advance, and only here does the church momentarily renounce its tensions to rejoice over lone victory won. Let me show you what I mean:

Thin, spare, and gray with the look of eagles and an air of restless patience, he sat on the second row, end seat, the first time I preached in the Austin pulpit. At the close of the sermon he put his long arms around me and called me to be his last pastor.

We had much in common in spite of the difference in our ages. He had heard John R. Sampey meet his first class in Hebrew, and sixty years later I had heard Sampey lead his last one. People looked at us in disbelief when he said that he, at eighty-four, and I, at thirty-two, had had the same great teacher.

In the years that were given to us much followed. He came to live in one of our church apartments, like old Eli in the temple. Though his children claimed he needed their homes and gladly urged him to come, he stayed where his heart had been for more than seventy years. Every day I learned more of the tensions, the conflicts, the devotion, the coming victory.

Rejected over his work with the Negro race; patronized for his early work with the Spanish-speaking; exhausted in labor over new churches born from Waco to Laredo and from Corpus Christi to Amarillo; victim of Indian arrows at lonely houses; often spending a day and a night on horseback to preach one time, three days by buggy to some Association, up and down the river's watershed, at last he bore the proud title "Prophet of the Pedernales."

A lost little son on the mesa, the death of his beloved, denominational controversy and struggle, integrity, character—all these were incidents of the journey to be lived through with firmness tempered with grace. Old age now came up behind him; children gone, his work done, it was time to relax.

But there was new need for old hands and heart. Mind open, eye quick to see, powerful in prayer, wise in counsel, he walked by my side daily through long, tension-ridden years. He knew my every thought and purpose; he shared every burden, while with delight in his presence I protested the consumption of his precious strength.

One day he came to my study with a few trinkets in his hands— some things he thought I would want—and that day he talked of his coming glory. Three weeks ahead and perfectly well, he knew. When I spoke to him of earthly things we shared, his mind was somewhere else.

I got to the hospital in time for his benediction that night. What he said to me is mine; but as he turned to marble in front of me, there was still the look of an old eagle and something eternal about him. I remembered his tensions over lesser gods, his conflict in the stream of the limited redemptions that surrounded, his constant pressures from life's lesser callings—and I saw his ultimate victory. There in the marbled form I saw his ultimate release from the tensions of the advance through storm, and it was wonderful.

What made my heart hurt so and hot tears scald my eyes the day I led his body out of the church while the great organ thundered "Hallelujah"? As the bass pedals rumbled over "He shall reign for ever and ever" in sixteen-foot open diapason, what made me want to sing? Why did my spine tingle in awe and a feeling of majesty when the woodwinds, strings, and brasses began the cry—

"Hallelujah! Hallelujah!
For the Lord God Omnipotent reigneth."

What held us all so rapt in wonder? Was it because we had seen in dying flesh "the victory that overcomes the world, even faith"? Was it because we had seen the church in momentary repose, freed from its tensions, while one of its own received the consummation?

"I've had all I can take of change and revolution. Throughout this terrible, so-called twentieth century, it's all I've seen, heard, read, and felt."

On the other hand, "Life *is* strife," they say Gautama Buddha has said.

And what if, Christianly, for all priests, change and conversion, rebellion and revolution are written in?

More—and much more gladly—what if change and revolution are our only paths to *revelation?*

Revelation? What has that to do with change and revolution! This is God's means of showing himself to us in Jesus Christ. He gets in us, and with respect to him we live a continuous conversion during a continuous revolution, says Richard Niebuhr. He puts everything under judgment. He demands a change of quest.

So: when you are in processes of change, under a judging, loving demand that makes you stand for and against—with some of your old ends slipping away—

Huge, beautiful and black, he threw his arms around me in front of the old Austin Hotel. Ten years before, during the struggles, we had had to go six blocks down Sixth Street to get coffee in a Mexican dive. "Now," he pronounced, *"things have changed here!"*

This is conversion; during a revolution, that may be revelation.

6

CHANGE AND REVOLUTION

I

"In every age," says Gustav Weigel, "the institutions (of religion) are dying."[1] He then adds, "They never do."

That they do not die our lives attest; and even our contemporary celebration of the secularity of our cities has become a dance we do around a modified altar. Old memories live in a race-unconscious that none of our brighter analysis has emptied. The gods do not die; they wait offstage to turn a new secularity into an older dance around an altar. Even the rationale of all the sources of our faiths does not dispose of the "will to believe" and we still lift our ceremonial cups at one commune or another in tribute to a Divine whose face we cannot see, suspecting that our blindness is ours.

Like everything else that lives long, the institutions of religion survive by their powers of accommodation.

So the Roman Church is not dying yet. Still the ghost of the Roman Empire, with all the laggard luggage of medievalism trailing, somewhat a stranger in the present age where church institutions are much more likely to house the ghost of business enterprise, she meets in Vatican II to change as little as she must and as much as she dares.

She sets us progressive Protestants on our ears; she seizes from our nervous hands the fraying banner of our limited ecumenism and passes us by. She meets in Council; invites us to watch her change as she must to live, through proper channels—and through the sainthood, if not godhood, of a beautiful, portly, old Italian peasant may even invite us all to the table, the Lord's table, where her belief in consecrated dough may modify to meet our common hunger for the Presence. She has changed some.

And so will we change some—four hundred years late. For as Harnack cites it, *"La médiocrité fonde l'autorité."* [2] Mediocrity breeds authority and all religious people would prefer an ordinance to a gospel. When will we ever learn it; the church lives by its changes! Pastors come and go; congregations grow up, die, are buried, and keep starting over again. Forms of worship change; denominational titles and groupings change; theological families have new children born or adopt others. All victories and defeats mean change of some kind.

Look at the changes we have endured: Christianity had first to overcome in the wide world that Jesus was a Jew and it still has to work at swallowing this. There was a victory to be won over her own adherents and her own origins. Meanwhile, the Empire, the Greek mind, competing religions, and Gnosticism were doing about as much to the Christian community as the community was doing to them. But she lived and throve through six centuries of definition (the great General Councils which hammered out Christian orthodoxy). She survived the Mohammedan hammer. The Muslim armies all but took Europe via Spain and again against Eastern Europe to the doors of Vienna. She lived with amazing ignorance in science, superstition in theology, and impiety in her clergy especially during the eleventh, twelfth, and thirteenth centuries. She put millions of Europeans on more or less stupid Crusades toward change. These crusades involved millions. Overall there were more than a dozen armies of considerable size and many smaller ones during the three-hundred-year period. One of the most tragic was the so-called Children's Crusade in which ten thousand disappeared into slavery. She gagged but swallowed a new view of the universe (Copernicus); a new definition

of method (Descartes to Darwin);[3] a new definition of man
(Nietzsche, Freud, and Marx);[4] a new definition of matter
(Einstein);[5] the triumph of physics;[6] and she lives now with the
coming triumph of the chemists which dwarfs anything we have seen,
for by it the final ropes of our mooring to the Stone Age are being cast
off in a new release from the land (Henri Breuil, Teilhard de Chardin
et al).

Through all these changes we have changed. As one church
historian put it long ago—the history of the church is the story of the
gospel's effect on the world and the world's effect on the gospel.
Through it all, there are some things all of us should know by now:

> *All dogma is constructed.*
> *All revelation is through human experience.*
> *All form is both sustenance and threat.*
> *All power is mediated authority.*
> *All freedom is limited.*

THE CHRISTIAN ESSENTIAL

The one essential that defines the church we may never have truly
caught. Without it we are never the church. It has never depended
upon agreement in evolution, physics, biology, chemistry, or
sociology. It exists the same for Jew or Ethiop, Roman or Russian,
Creek or Choctaw. It doesn't matter whether we are rationalists,
irrationalists, determinists, or poets. The concern even to have a
relevant cosmology is irrelevant. No Christian insight rests on a
timeless unchanging cosmology.[7] To all the ways of looking at our
universe the church must adjust as it and they go—around a common
essential.

Some have said this essential is love, or humility, or compassion, or
mercy. Our Master had in mind not just an ethic or a quality, but a
relation. Richard Niebuhr says that *we are, in the Gospels, impressed
not that Jesus loved, or was humble, or merciful.[8] It was that he loved
the Father. He loved God radically, and Him he radically obeyed.*
One hundred eighty verses in John's Gospel alone are in the context

of this obsession. There is no legitimate way to talk about Jesus Christ apart from his obsession with what Niebuhr has called *radical monotheism.* We are, he says, not called to love our neighbor as we love God, but as we love ourselves. We are to love God as we love nothing else. The church rests on this. And mercy, justice, compassion, and humility? They all proceed from the love of the Father. The Christian unchanging is that in Jesus Christ men come to know their Father whose mercy and love they reflect. Everything else changes. When we enter this love relationship with the Father, here alone, we are in the church.

THE ROMANTIC TEMPTATION

Someone told Thomas Carlyle that George Eliot had decided to accept the universe. "Gad, she'd better!" And this universe knows change, tension, strife, decay, and some progress as its daily bread. Tension holds the universe in its station. "Life is strife" someone says in English, then claims we learned this not from Darwin but from Gautama Buddha who later died of a strife in his belly caused by eating too much bad pork. Yet we never really learn that life is strife; and because this is so, Whitehead says that the major advances of civilization are processes which all but wreck the societies in which they occur.[9]

The great temptation for religion is always the romantic temptation: e.g., we try to live in a world that never was or one that is already dead. Heinrich Heine once reported the annual appointment of a pair of beadles at Gottingen to be sure no new ideas were smuggled into the university! One of our very favorite ways of escape from today's bad world is to cluster in houses designed to permit recovery of happier days of yore. Says Shirley Jackson Case, ". . . we strive only for a life of imitative mediocrity."[10] And, some things change very little. A prisoner, accused of heresy before the *Inquisitores,* testified: "I am not a heretic; I eat meat, I lie, I curse, and am a faithful Christian." Yet, meanwhile, we know: *All forms develop in particular settings. None can be expected to remain unchanged.* Fosdick used to remind us that the one real heresy was the belief that we have reached finality in a settled system. Meanwhile we long, we nostalgically long, for that "third kind of church"[11] for which, says Harnack, the Western nations wait.

A GROSSER ERROR—IRRESISTIBLE PROGRESS

There is a grosser sin than the quest for changelessness. This would be the old faith in irresistible progress. We really do have to make our way from here, carving our destiny from a jungle.

> Upon the basis of a scientific doctrine of evolution, no idolatrous superstition could be much more lacking in intellectual support than Spencer's confidence in a universal, mechanical, irresistible movement towards perfection.[12]

History is the Fury, *Alecto;*[13] she rises and falls at the same time. Augustine writes *De Civitate Dei (The City of God),* with Alaric in Rome and Genseric soon to besiege the Hippo where Augustine was pastor.[14] Jerome weeps as he translates Holy Scripture, "They say Rome the Queen has fallen!"[15] Nothing the Middle Ages thought to be eternal has survived as a world power of first rank—neither its astronomy, nor its empire, nor its church, nor its teacher, Aquinas. Human history is a tortured mountain path, and all progress means sense and change and work. But history rises and falls. An archaeologist says the guide who took him to the site of the greatest university of the ancients could not himself read and had never known anyone who could! Progress involves a tragic, ceaseless round of war against decay.

Over against the immoral insomnia of our wait for irresistible progress stands the ungodly anxiety of a human quest for changelessness. The desire for a static faith and a permanent house that guarantees the intimate presence of the Eternal is the desire to be as God. It is to deny our human finitude. To crave changelessness is not only impossibility; it is immoral. This is to crave death. It represents a middle-aged mind that no one wishes back, for it died once. This kind of static faith would require the suffocation of intelligence, the emasculation of reason, such rigidity of institution as to guarantee burial of freedom and the death of all inquiry. We Christians are a "pilgrim people" or we are dead. We have to remember Abraham who "sought a city" all his life (Hebrews 11:10) or lose our character.

Faith is still as it was—dynamic and paradoxical. It can and it cannot. Every day the believer must be born again and resume his journey. Every old answer is forbidden, until some present urgency makes it new. Faith, says Sören Kierkegaard, is a deep and blessed unrest. It urges the believer on. No rest here! Or he ceases to be a believer, and he never can sit on a staff he will not use for travel. And over this pilgrim people, if God speaks, he never bellows and his peace may seldom descend, for the goal is not peace, but manhood; and if there is peace at all in that occasional Interpreters' House [16] in a secular city, where is the peace?

If it comes for the moment at all, it will be the temporary peace of seeing a glimpse of all parts in the light of a whole, a universal sacrament, as William Temple [17] and Teilhard de Chardin, [18] both understand. It will be a celebration, some high Mass or other which may come in the absence of all houses and altars so long as there is earth to offer oneself upon. [19] If there is a peace, it will come as one sees himself an instrument in the hands of the Eternal, being pointed at and sharpened for the making of a social and personal righteousness. The peace will not be that of a defended fortress.

Pierre Teilhard de Chardin has moved me as no other Catholic writer of our time: "What we are up against is the heavy swell of an unknown sea which we are just entering from behind the cape that has protected us." [20] He joins Henri Breuil in claiming that we have just cast off the last moorings which held us to the neolithic age. It matters very much, he thinks, that we should learn that at the price we are paying life is taking a mighty step in us and in our setting. He sees a critical change in the sphere of the mind during these post-Renaissance years—a change as critical for our future as that explosive change from a 300cc to a 12-1500cc brain case in our species. He feels that something big is coming off here. Abraham Maslow calls it "full-humanization." [21] And, since mid-nineteenth century we should have been able to see "the *irreversible coherence* of all that exists." [22] This is a true Catholicism. For, blind, deaf, and dumb are we who do not see the sweep of a movement whose track runs so far beyond us. All human knowledge is involved. It represents a general condition to which all theories and movements are liable and viable.[23] Modern man is the fellow who knows this and can include himself as an agent and factor in these processes of change. Progress is never automatic, but there is here begotten a new hope that man may yet be Man.

IN THE JUNGLE OF OUR SECULARITY

All this, in the jungle of our secularity, forces us to look to what remains of the tools we have been bequeathed to use on our journey. All this, heard and swallowed, sends us in—and out—of such Interpreters' House as we can find in our pilgrimage with Abraham, *et alii,* to some City of Light which for now, for us, is still a "City in the Wilderness." And here our old men may still help us—and here, midway in his great powers, Adolf Harnack had come on his journey that day more than sixty years ago—

> The man of any deep feeling will thankfully receive anything that the development of progress may bring him; but he knows very well that his situation inwardly—the problems that agitate him and the fundamental position in which he stands—is not . . . altered by it all.[24]

Then (and I have lived by this for all my years since twenty),

> Gentlemen, when a man grows older . . . he does not find, if he possesses any inner world at all, that he is advanced by the external march of things, by "the progress of civilization." Nay, he feels himself, rather, where he was before, and forced to seek the sources of strength which his forefathers also sought. He is forced to make himself a native of the kingdom of God, the kingdom of the Eternal, the kingdom of Love; and he comes to understand that it was only of this kingdom that Jesus Christ desired to speak and to testify, and he is grateful to him for it.[25]

TO LIVE BETWEEN THE TIMES

Our priestly narrative and language, properly heard, understands and thrives on change. There is hardly a static or functional phrase in the memory of the people whose interpretation of their common experience made the Book. Look at the complex of resurrection "memories" to see what I mean. Luke 24 is a good source of them.

Here is a typical one: ". . . and their eyes were opened and they recognized him; and he vanished out of their sight" (Luke 24:31, RSV).

Practically no one had ever had these problems before. Although resurrection had changed things unbelievably, they had still a problem that had marked their relations to him from the beginning: They had to live between his comings and his goings. They could not lay hold on him solidly. He could never be held in their grasp. The cross was the only place they had ever seen him *fixed*. Now resurrection had changed all that. It was as before—they were back to living between the times of his manifestation.

Disconcerting, to say the least, never to know around what corner you will go head-on into Messiah! Disconcerting, this: to be talking to a rank stranger for hours on the road; to sit with him at meat, your heart burning over something you cannot identify; then, to see him break and hear him bless your bread—and recognize *Messiah!* Only to have him gone again! Does He never stay? Well, what *do* you think the point really is in all those "memories" of theirs about after the cross?

Disconcerting, to be called "Mary" in a cemetery where you've gone to mourn; to find a folded headcloth, but no *body;* to hear him say, "Hail, all," or call for some cooked fish; or to hear him come through your door, saying, "Peace," as if he had not just died! Or to have him invite you to touch him, since you cannot believe without it, but then, he disappears. Disconcerting, at the least, to have him feed you breakfast, walk you down the beach, and say right to your face, "Do you love me?"—and, ask it three times over with you answering as hard as you can all the while!

Messiahs ought not to be so unpredictable—much less ordinary people. (Tolstoi said he simply could not stand that man Gogol; he would walk right up to you in a group of men and ask if you *really* love your wife.) It is acutely disconcerting with Messiahs not to be able to expect according to a schedule of times and seasons. It is too upsetting when the other is unpredictable, inexplicable, but overpowering. So they lived between the times of his comings to them and his going from them—and this is a meaning of their memories.

Had it not always been this way? They could never apprehend *him;* he was always apprehending them, seizing a man against his better judgment, compelling: in the temple court, at Capernaum, or when he infected the swine on the hill and wasn't even on hand to be billed for the damage. Or when he came to them across the water after feeding the thousands; or at Solomon's porch that day an angel really stirred the waters; or that time at the house of Zacchaeus; or that night with Simon the Pharisee and the harlot; always unpredictable, inexplicable. Disconcerting, never to know over what hilltop you could go head-on into some new demand from Messiah. (Simon, do you love me?)

"And in the breaking of bread, their eyes were opened, and they knew him, and he vanished out of their sight" (Luke 24:30-31).

Back across eight tortuous miles, breathless with *news,* to the upper room, only to be greeted, before they could blurt out *theirs,* by the *others* who said: "The Lord is risen indeed! *Simon* has seen him" (Luke 24:34). Living between his comings and goings was enough to break a man.

It still is. Who knows around what corner he will run head-on into some demand from Messiah? Who knows, in advance, which hymn, or set of eyes, or touch, or prayer will bear some new word of command from Messiah? A man has to be braced for this. If he can go meeting Messiah on any road; if any human voice can bear His call; if he is liable to keep on appearing to his own—a man had better be careful!

It is like waiting for the other shoe to fall. It is like living in terror of sharp corners lest you meet someone coming breakneck on a bicycle. It is terribly disconcerting and demanding to have Messiah—and no schedule. So much better, we say, if we could have kept him in his grave, or on the cross, or at least in the church where we could send for him when we want him. Or, modestly enough, we could keep him in the Supper's bread and wine, wrapped in napkin and chalice, lest he get loose in the town and choke us all with his demands on the neighbor. That unpredictable and off-schedule coming is terrible.

The early community had to learn to live between the times of

God's appearing. As they learned, several conditions of any coming became clear:

He never came and stayed long enough to take away their responsible initiative.

His manifestations of power never came as long as they had any strength of their own.

His coming never gave them a permanent advantage.

So they learned to live with, and wait for, his appearances.

We priests must live our changes between the times, too: this five-hundred-year transition from sensate to ideational culture, with no one yet sure just what is the big idea; or this transition from many worlds to one world, now more than two centuries on the road. Then there is this present between the times for the disadvantaged races, four hundred years on the road in this hemisphere; and this eight-hundred-year procession toward freedom more or less for ordinary menfolk, with vast new social changes happening faster than we can smear them with old labels. Underneath all this there is the necessity for moving from the world of Copernicus to the world seen at Palomar on clear nights—this new space world and these new Columbuses who bring back no word of cities of gold to make us really want to go there. And over it, this between the peace on a road to war; or a between the wars on a road to peace, whichever. The church always must live its changes in some betweentime—and this is the point for our hope. And so must you. But the message of the hope is still that your outside limits are not your birthday and death date. We live rather between *his* death and *our* resurrection.

How do we live between such times? The language of faith demands that we live expectantly, redemptively—as redeemers. This means we dare not commit the abomination and crime of marking off our own history. (Dear Luther thought the world would not make it through the sixteenth century since the world was aging faster than revelation. Edmund Spenser longed for what he called Sabaoth, the death of this world and the creation of a new, *changeless* and eternal: His last words in *The Faerie Queen,*

"O that great Sabaoth's God
Grant me that Sabaoth's sight.")

Positively or negatively, we have to live expectantly with change. The early church expected this coming across every hilltop. Paul's "We shall not all die" is authentic; as is Karl Barth's use of "every eye shall see. . . ." There is no hope in change without expecting. And how else can we, who do not yet trust each other, live redemptively?

Meanwhile, how does this living with change and revolution work itself out in the life of a single priest, himself supported by a company of changing revolutionaries who are priests, too? And what has all this to do with his expectancy of Revelation?

II

The revelation we have in Christianity is not our possession of a Person which leads to the development of religious ideas. It is rather a continuing conversion of our ideas with respect to the Person who judges and loves us. God's disclosure of himself, Christ in the world, is that permanent revolution in our religious life by which all our truths are painfully transferred and all behavior transfigured by continuing repentance and new faith. The Christian life is a life lived not before or after but during a great revolution.[26] A compulsion has been placed upon us. We are under the law to love.[27] A new beginning has been offered us which we cannot evade in Jesus Christ. God's love, power, and justice have been redisclosed. Life has been constituted around and in a revolution. At what points are you being converted? Where are you in revolution? This, says Richard Niebuhr, is your experience of revelation.

When I preached this hard and compelling doctrine in my own place, I closed with the question, "Where are *you* being converted?" Afterwords, at a forum, a dozen lay priests turned the tables on me:

"Reverend, we hear. Now tell us—at what points *are you* being converted with respect to Christ, and where are *you* in revolution?"

It's fair enough. And it is a basis of hope.

For some decades now the *Christian Century* has printed every ten years a series: "How My Mind Has Changed." It has been stimulating, even frightening, to see some of our great teachers change so.

Now a change of mind is not *per se* a conversion, though conversion will involve some changes of mind. Conversion is more: it is a deep metanoia (repentance) of being: a repentance of the very self-soul which is a turning wrongside out; a change of loyalty, direction, value, and concern, as well as a change of mind. But changes of mind are important. They may betoken conversions on the way. They may represent a deep development already in process. They represent growth, or decline, or aging. They deserve consideration in the hope that they may point to genuine conversion at a deeper level and a revolution in process at points that matter. In these twenty last years I have experienced some changes I believe to be representative of a conversion I am undergoing, during a revolution I am living:

I have changed my mind about what it is to be a good minister. One really needs to know less, talk less, remember little, and receive all the time. It doesn't take so much "smart," but calls for lots of sense.

My notions of what it is to be a preacher and the techniques of preaching have changed. It's all dialogue, really; mostly caricature; more question than answer; and their turning of the head is part of the conversation.

My images of a good senior minister are radically different now. It *really* matters that all the rest, lay especially, should have their ministry full-orbed. It's even all right to be a lousy administrator, to have to trust your brothers, to be "away," and to be "available" because they matter.

I've changed my mind about what is a good church meeting. Only two or three are needed, but always some eternally significant "yes" or "no."

My estimate of the real potential for church, the depths of concern, is vastly enlarged. The power of the church truly lies not where I thought it to lie; it shifts about wherever anyone is hearing and being heard—sometimes its real power is embodied in a child less than three years old. This is why you drop to your knee to seek his eye level. How else can he give you his power?

I have changed my mind about how communication happens and who is a communicator and what the barriers to communication are.[28] Indeed, I wonder at times that there is any at all! But I know now, with Reinhold Niebuhr, and against T. J. J. Altizer, that there is *always* a "penumbra of mystery" to faith. [29]

I know more now, I think, about how a person is put together and why he is as he is. And radically, my mind has changed about the bounds of my responsibility and the nature of my calling and service. I am not God; I do not have to "be a blessing"; I do not have to hear all who "offer" to talk, or make a demand. I can say "no" to those who threaten me overwhelmingly until we can find a better ground to talk on, and I may even send some empty away, for I have been emptied, too. A man does not have to lie—and salvation belongs to God.

I have changed my mind about who can be saved, about who is a teacher, and about from whom we can learn. The nature of guilt, mine and yours, is vastly extended. And I know more about the real possibility of a real health of soul.

My mind is at peace now about what kind of help we may expect from God and what kind we will never get. (It has been thirty years since I have asked God to "fix" anything in the South. He has a majority of Baptists-Methodists alone down here.)

My mind has changed about who is responsible (not always me!); about what is important in Christian education (no pre-set specifications, please); about the importance of language and the hard work of hearing; and about who is not an expert. I have discovered the difference between preaching and doing. Rasputin once said, "If I can I *do,* if I cannot, I preach!" I feel myself on the threshhold of the claim to some kind of manhood or "self-actualization" and I have begun to learn where God can be met with in the world!

Now these are mere changes of mind. I believe they rise from a conversion during a revolution still proceeding. That is to say, I believe I am under Revelation and that I am being converted, and I know I am in revolt.

CONVERSION TO FAITH

I speak of my conversion with respect to *faith* and its limits. I must make a fundamental concession to knowledge. I simply do not *know*.

The Christian is agnostic. This means an acceptance of my ignorance (not a peace, but a truce). I am still a victim of theological lust. I want to know, but I do not know. I am *docta ignorantia* (teacher of ignorance),[30] and the limits of my knowledge lie closer into shore than I like. This is a confession of my limits, and the "new math," or any other, confounds me, for I am really a pre-Copernican man. But this conversion means more than that. It means the discovery that faith *in the passive voice alone* (reform-theology in the main) is a blind guide which has little if any responsible help to give me. It means the discovery that faith *in the active voice* is the demand for obedience to light I already have. It means the discovery of the validity of my "ministry of error."[31] Not much really depends upon my being *right*. It means I do now submit to a demand—a transcendental demand—on the part, to serve a Whole I can neither contain nor express. It means I am member to a species which has a very limited life cycle and capacity within that cycle. It means I have not very far to go. And, it means I have begun the visceral acceptance of symbols I cannot improve, such as cross, bread, wine, and water. It really means a continuing conversion to Jesus Christ as Lord. After thirty-five years of it I can really find no other to follow. This is a repeating confirmation.

CONVERSION OF DESPAIR

The conversion of my despair began at its intersection with a hope. Where despair and hope intersect, I am being saved, still. This intersection is *the* ground of existentialism, and I do not abandon that ground or the posture, but my wallow in despair is over. I have been met with a hope. Faith, in the active voice, which is *work,* is really obedience, the ground of hope. On this Arminian modification of native reformed soil,[32] I can stand. On my more nearly obedient days I have tasted a recovery of nerve which is a manhood in the ministry. This means one can speak up! This issues in a recovery of meaning known only to personal theologians or theological persons and produces the prospect of a recovery of communion, the church in your own house.

Do you see? I am really speaking of a conversion toward manhood.

(In these preacher schools they look at me as if I were sick sometimes when I say we need our manhood more than we need to be ministers.) I mean by this that I was forced to an acceptance of guilt, my guilt, and more—of my shame. My teachers here were Hobart Mowrer and a twelve-year-old after communicants' class:

> "What is guilt, little girl?" I had asked her, thinking I knew. *"Guilt is a shame you can talk about,"* she answered. "And what is shame?" Head low, eyes averted, but lifted toward the Kortheuer *Crucifixion* on my wall and the spectator-figure of despair with which we both had identified, she said, *"Shame is a guilt you can't talk about."* And we let the matter go.

The conversion of manhood begins here for me in the acceptance of my guilt-ness. Where all are guilty, none is guilty. I meet a new notion of redemption in the child. It's all right to be guilty lest I lose my brother who is guilty, too. There is a Korean GI word for this. We are *samo-samo;* and there is no brotherhood of redemption which is not a brotherhood of guilt as well. It's all right for things to be this way.

All of which has showed me how far we have to go. I am on some days aghast at the rooms upstairs still unoccupied, at the waste areas still unclaimed, at the ghastly power of sin, evil, and my own unconscious and conscious capacity for both; and I throw up after meetings with the shallow pretensions of us professional churchmen. But these very points—a hope—I am being saved by the Christ, by you, and by my brothers. And the revolution?

REVOLUTION AGAINST DENOMINATION

Here I confess I am *Der Mensch im Widerspruch*—Man in Revolt,[33] against my denomination—except that now it hardly matters any more. It mattered once, for we had our great chances.

First in the American church to sense the worth of Biblical Criticism, twenty years before Goodspeed at Chicago, Crawford Toy was fired in 1871 at Louisville for seeing and saying that religious language was language, too, and must therefore be treated as language. (It took six pages of Harvard Faculty Minutes to record their tribute at his death years later.)

Earliest of his compeers to see that religious history is history, too, and must be treated as history, was W. H. Whitsett. He was exiled from his presidency of Southern Baptist Seminary at Louisville (1901).

Second only to the great Presbyterian Woodrow at Columbia, E. Y. Mullins[34] introduced us to psychology and evolution but accepted virtual repudiation in the Memphis Confession[35] as late as 1926.

Brightest light in the world of his generation in terms of social compassion, Walter Rauschenbusch could stomach his Southern compeers for less than a year. Dead, cremated, and scattered over a little Canadian lake, fifty years since his death, he is anathema still to his brothers, except here and there.

We were great in educational potential, but McGlothlen, likely the best historian of Christian thought in the South, who saw our Reformation origins, has been swamped in the sludge of Landmarkism.[36]

Great in evangelistic concern, John Buchanan, leader in a move to bring Southern Baptists into closer world-church connection, was buried under a wave of repudiation of the world-church. Add to all this the Huguenot Expulsion[37] that has marked us since the forties, the confidence in "controlled ignorance" and functionalistic methodologies, the egoistic absurdities and isolationisms, and it means that I can name more than forty men, who represent more than two centuries of graduate study in Europe's best universities, who hold no longer any connection whatever, except nostalgic memory, with the institutions that sired, hired, and fired them. Every seminary and graduate school I know in the North and East has its refugees from among the Baptists in the South. This is our best and *only* contribution to the world-church. There is no excuse for us. We are the people who never heard our teachers. We are God's most provincial people!

Unless it be that we Lutherans are the worst; or we Methodists, or the Presbyterians South of the Smith and Wesson line, or we Episcopalians. What a flock of regional fundamentalists our forms and frames cover here.

There must be another day somewhere for these old adjectives. I am in revolt against them all. They are mere bookkeeping devices to protect the vested interests. They are no longer salt. But there is a larger and more important revolt to join. The denominations are dead. Except for certain bookkeeping capacities, no *real* distinctives separate Christians anymore. Let the denominations go—and join the revolt that really matters.

THE REVOLT AGAINST IGNORANCE

There is, I say, a broader sedition to join. It is the revolt against our own ignorance, lethargy, our self-complacent images, our myth systems of the self, the piety of all mere regionalisms and Bible Belts—the casting off of what we know to be pious humbug. We all teach less than we know!

Eight sets of myths surround and proscribe every attempt at adult Christian education in the American church. There simply is no way to come at the Christian education of adults except through a frontal assault on these myth sets. It does no good to say the future of the church is its youth! For this is an evasive lie. The *future* of the church is its present adult generation. And here, in the thirties and forties, prime years, they are eaten out with the kind of congenital conservatism that will corrode our pipes for another long generation without a frontal assault on the myth sets that support the value structure they have built into a tepee outside of which they never have to go. In here, wrapped in their blankets of shallow goals and goods, they are virtually impregnable and worse, impenetrable, unless a visiting fireman happens to mention Vietnam, Cuba, American exploitation, or the Klan. (I could not have looked to *these* to integrate our church. It takes the *old* men for this bloody business. So one returns to the real liberals, the old veterans, the founder fathers who will cry and protest and sign and fight it through because it is right.)[38] There is no hope for those people in the thirties and forties unless we face the myths. And this means conflict, without which there is no change, without which there has been no Christian education.

The myths? I mean, first, the myth about *property,* and the absurd notion under it that *poverty* is the opposite. The terms "property" and "poverty" are more nearly homonomous than heteronomous. They are synonyms. The opposite of both is *community.*

Second, I mean the myth about *character,* which most of us think we have had forever, but hardly dare scratch more than forty years behind us, lest we find a refugee from some British or German cannibalism. The myth about a character we largely never had, when added to the myth about property, adds up to the myth of the *good life,* which ends, too, and too soon in "little boxes, little boxes."

I mean, third, the myth about *race, racial origins,* and native *intelligence.* I mean the myth about *patria,* one's native land and region and its vaunted superiorities. I mean the *religious* myth, and the *sex-difference* myth, and the *political-economic* myth, and the myth that I do not have to die. No way—there is simply no way to maturity except directly through these sets of fabrications designed to protect self-soul from the realities of suffering and evil—against which we are called to revolt, too, lest they smother us and we die.

This is the language of discernment and revelation that I hear and try to speak. It has bred in me a hope—a tragic hope and a real one. Lived out, it means we are longing for a new *expectancy* to match our long memory. Lived out, it means the recovery of the Jewish hope. Realized, the meaning of this language is the salvation of the world. It means to look for Messiah—for the coming of the kingdom of the Lord. And this is what the Christian means when really praising God.

NOTES

Introduction

[1] This Introduction is based on chapter 20 of Carlyle Marney, *The Coming Faith* (Nashville: Abingdon Press, 1970). The information in this Introduction is completely recast with new material added. Nevertheless, several paragraphs of the earlier version are quoted verbatim. Permission from Abingdon Press is acknowledged with appreciation.

[2] Private correspondence received by the author from Stewart Newman, 1973.

[3] Ernest G. Schwiebert, *Luther and His Times* (St. Louis: Concordia Publishing House, 1950), p. 473.

[4] Referred to in Schwiebert, *op. cit.,* p. 443.

[5] Graydon E. McClellan, "The Ministry," *New Frontiers of Christianity,* ed. Ralph C. Raughley, Jr. (New York: Association Press, 1962), p. 129.

[6] Martin Luther, "To Elector Frederick, March 5, 1522" *Luther's Works* (Philadelphia: Fortress Press, 1963), vol. 48, p. 397.

[7] *Ibid.,* p. 391. (Italics author's.)

[8] For analysis of this often denied but more often affirmed story, see Erik Erikson, *Young Man Luther* (New York: W. W. Norton & Company, Inc., 1958), pp. 23-48.

[9] Martin Luther, "The Misuse of the Mass," *Luther's Works* (Philadelphia: Muhlenberg Press, 1959), vol. 36, p. 202.

[10] Martin Luther, *Church and Ministry, Luther's Works,* ed. Helmut T. Lehmann and Conrad Bergendoff (Philadelphia: Muhlenberg Press, 1958), vol. 40, p. 8. Reprinted by permission of Fortress Press, Philadelphia.

[11] *Ibid.,* pp. 9-10.

[12] Martin Luther, "Exposition of Psalm 110:4," *Selected Psalms,* ed., Jaroslav Pelikan, *Luther's Works* (St. Louis: Concordia Publishing House, 1956), vol. 13, p. 330. See also pp. 309-334.

[13] Martin Luther, *Church and Ministry,* ed. Helmut T. Lehmann and Conrad Bergendoff, *op. cit.,* p. 21. See also Matin Luther, *The Babylonian Captivity, Captivity of the Church.*

[14] *Ibid.,* p. 19.

[15] Martin Luther, "Exposition of Psalm 110:4" *op. cit.,* p. 332.

[16] Martin Luther, "To the Illustrious Senate and People of Prague," *Luther's Works* (Philadelphia: Muhlenberg Press, 1958), vol. 40, pp. 7-44.

[17] Gibson Winter, *The New Creation As Metropolis* (New York: The Macmillan Company, 1963).

[18] *Ibid.,* pp. 8-9.

[19] *Ibid.,* pp. 9-10.

[20] John Bunyan, *Pilgrim's Progress.*

[21] Martin Luther, *The Sermon on the Mount,* ed., Jaroslav Pelikan, *Luther's Works* (St. Louis: Concordia Publishing House, 1956), vol. 21. See also Gustaf Wingren, *Luther on Vocation* (Philadelphia: Fortress Press, 1957).

Chapter One: The Christian Genius

[1] In Carlyle Marney, *Structures of Prejudice* (Nashville: Abingdon Press, 1961), pp. 23-53, in my treatment of materialism, I gave "matter" too little room; and now I insist that fundamental Jewish insight into *creation* takes matter much more seriously.

[2] See Denis De Rougemont, *Man's Western Quest,* trans. Montgomery Belgion, vol. 13 of *World Perspectives,* ed. Ruth Nanda Anshen (New York: Harper & Row, Publishers, 1957). This book stands as a source for much that follows in chapter 1.

[3] The religion of Mani, a contrast between Light and Dark, Spirit and Matter, matter being the abode of all evil, was a spectacular rival of early Christianity. Augustine, in his twenty-ninth year, claimed victory over its restrictions, moved into incarnational Christianity, and wrote some half dozen works against the Manichee.

[4] De Rougemont, *op. cit.,* p. 23.

[5] Reference here is to the great General Councils of the Church: Nicaea, A.D. 325; Constantinople, A.D. 381; Ephesus, A.D. 431; Chalcedon, A.D. 451; Constantinople II, A.D. 553; Constantinople III, A.D. 680; Nicaea II, A.D. 787. My claim is that all the talk about "persons" in the Godhead is really best understood as a concern with man, but no then-known "psychology" could have made this clear.

[6] Sermon by Samuel Miller, then Dean of Harvard Divinity School.

[7] See John MacMurray, *The Clue to History* (New York: Harper & Row, Publishers, 1939).

[8] See Charles N. Cochrane, *Christianity and Classical Culture* (New York: Oxford University Press, Inc., 1957), especially chapters 1, 2, 3, 4.

[9] See MacMurray, *op. cit.,* pp. 16-41; and Joseph Klausner, *Jesus to Paul* (New York: The Macmillan Company, 1944), books I and II.

[10] See Christopher Dawson, *Religion and Culture* (New York: Sheed & Ward, Inc., 1948); and *Religion and the Rise of Western Culture* (New York: Sheed & Ward, Inc., 1950).

[11] Mircea Eliade, *Cosmos and History,* trans. Willard Trask (New York: Harper & Row, Publishers, 1959), pp. 161f.

[12] Hugh K. MacKintosh, *Types of Modern Theology* (New York: Charles Scribner's Sons, 1937), pp. 63-64.

[13] See John MacMurray, *The Self as Agent* (London: Faber and Faber Limited, 1957); and *Persons in Relation* (New York: Humanities Press, Inc., 1970), especially vol. 1, chapters 1, 3, 4.

[14] See Dawson, *Religion and the Rise of Western Culture,* chapters 2, 4, 11.

[15] See John MacMurray, *The Self as Agent,* pp. 17-38.

[16] See Frederick Denison Maurice, *Theological Essays* (London: Macmillan & Co., Ltd., 1891).

[17] Karl Barth, *The Humanity of God* (Richmond: John Knox Press, 1960), pp. 37-65. See also Karl Barth, *Christ and Adam* (New York: The Macmillan Company).

Chapter Two: The Grammar of Faith

[1] Franklin Littell, *From State Church to Pluralism* (Garden City, N.Y.: Doubleday & Company, Inc., Anchor Books edition, 1962).

[2] The reference is to Deuteronomy 23:1, "He that is wounded in the stones or has his privy member cut off, shall not enter into the assembly of Yahweh."

[3] Martin Buber, *I and Thou* (New York: Charles Scribner's Sons, 1958), p. 5.

[4] Floyd V. Filson, *Studies in Biblical Theology* (London: SCM Press Ltd., n. d.). In essence this sentence is a condensation of eight principles by which I have for thirty years evaluated any Christian teaching offered to me as "Christian."

[5] See Kenneth J. Foreman, *Identification: Human and Divine* (Richmond: John Knox Press, 1963).

[6] See Soren Kierkegaard, *The Sickness Unto Death,* trans. Walter Lowrie (Princeton, N. J.: Princeton University Press, 1954).

[7] See Paul Scherer, *Event in Eternity* (New York: Harper & Row, Publishers, 1945); and *For We Have This Treasure* (New York: Harper & Row, Publishers, 1944).

Chapter Three: The Recovery of Form and Shape

[1] See H. Richard Niebuhr, *Christ and Culture* (New York: Harper & Row, Publishers, 1951). Now more than twenty years old, and as fresh as when I first heard these ideas, Niebuhr's book offers a descriptive methodology for the life of Christians vis à vis culture that is still definitive and vital.

[2] George Santayana, *Winds of Doctrine* (New York: Charles Scribner's Sons, 1926), p. 1. (Italics added.) Reprinted by permission of J. M. Dent & Sons, Ltd., London. The following short quotations are also from this source.

[3] *Ibid.* (Italics added.)

[4] *Ibid.,* p. 2.

[5] See Schubert Ogden, *Christ Without Myth* (New York: Harper & Row, Publishers, 1961).

[6] G. Ernest Wright, *God Who Acts* (London: SCM Press, Ltd., 1952), p. 22.

[7] Other phrases used to describe this concept are "self-actualization, full-humanness." See Abraham Maslow, *Toward a Psychology of Being* (New York: Van Nostrand Reinhold Company, 1962); and *Motivation and Personality* (New York: Harper & Row, Publishers, 1957).

[8] See Pierre Teilhard de Chardin, *The Divine Milieu* (New York: Harper & Row, Publishers, 1960).

[9] Arnold Come, *Agents of Reconciliation* (Philadelphia: The Westminster Press, 1960), p. 12.

[10] Franklin Littell, *From State Church to Pluralism* (Garden City, N.Y.: Doubleday & Company, Inc., Anchor Books edition, 1962), p. 32.

[11] See Howard Mumford Jones, *O Strange New World* (New York: The Viking Press, Inc., 1964), especially chapters 5, 6, and 10.

[12] See Pitirim A. Sorokin, *The Crisis of Our Age* (New York: E. P. Dutton & Co., Inc., 1942), chap. 5, for a sophisticated and learned analysis of modernity. See also Joseph Wood Krutch, *Human Nature and the Human Condition* (New York: Random House, Inc., 1959).

[13] George F. Kennan, *American Diplomacy* (New York: Mentor Books, 1951), especially chapters 1, 3.

[14] See Kenneth Scott Latourette, *A History of the Expansion of Christianity* (New York: Harper & Row, Publishers, 1944), vol. 6, pp. 65-214.

[15] See Frederick Herzog, *Liberation Theology* (New York: The Seabury Press, Inc., 1972). This is a theology designed to escape the limits of adjectival modifiers, such as white, black, Southern "theologies."

[16] See William Graham Sumner, *Folkways* (Boston: Ginn and Company, 1940). See also William E. H. Lecky, *A History of European Morals* (New York: Appleton-Century-Crofts, 1927), 2 volumes.

[17] See Charles Norris Cochrane, *Christianity and Classical Culture* (New York: Oxford University Press, Inc., 1957).

[18] "The First Apology of Justin," *The Apostolic Fathers with Justin Martyr and Irenaeus,* The Ante-Nicene Fathers (Grand Rapids, Mich.: Wm. B. Eerdmans Publishing Company, 1967), vol. 1., p. 167.

Chapter Four: The Nerve to Submit

[1] Karl Barth, *Church Dogmatics,* vol. 3, part 2 of *The Doctrine of Creation* (Edinburgh: T. & T. Clark, 1960), pp. 114-115. The paragraph closes with "The Lord was not in the storm, the earthquake or the fire. (1 Kings 19:11f). He really was not."

[2] See Loren Eiseley, *The Immense Journey* (New York: Random House, Inc., 1957); and *The Unexpected Universe* (New York: Harcourt Brace Jovanovich, Inc., 1969).

[3] Robert A. Raines, *Creative Brooding* (New York: The Macmillan Company, 1966), p. 13.

[4] This insight of contemporary sociology lies at the base of the work of Lecky, Sumner, Durkheim, Wundt, Odum, and others.

[5] Edwin McNeill Poteat, *Mandate to Humanity* (Nashville: Abingdon Press, 1953), p. 76. (Italics added.)

[6] A classic translation from Hassidic Jewry of the late nineteenth century.

[7] Paul Tournier, *The Meaning of Persons* (New York: Harper & Row, Publishers, 1957), p. 204.

[8] At the close of the debates Luther consented (Oct. 4, 1959) to the statement of fourteen "Articles of Marburg." Later developed by Melanchthon and others, the effective transition in a great spiritual movement from "credo" to "creed" was determined.

[9] Loren Eiseley, *The Immense Journey,* pp. 47-49.

[10] See Paul L. Lehmann, *Ethics in a Christian Context* (New York: Harper & Row, Publishers, 1963), pp. 74-101.

[11] *Ibid.,* p. 101.

[12] *Ibid.*

Chapter Five: Conflict and Tension

[1] William M. Dixon, *The Human Situation* (London: Longmans Green, n. d.), p. 197. Reprinted by permission of Edward Arnold Ltd., London.

[2] *Ibid.*

[3] *Ibid.*

[4] Nicolas Berdyaev, *The Destiny of Man* (London: Geoffrey Bles, n. d.), pp. 28f.

[5] *Ibid.*

[6] Dixon, *op. cit.,* p. 50.

[7] *Ibid.,* p. 90.

[8] *Ibid.*

[9] See Paul Scherer, *Event in Eternity* (New York: Harper & Row, Publishers, 1945).

[10] Pitirim Sorokin, *Social and Cultural Dynamics* (New York: American Book Company, 1941) and *The Crisis of Our Age* (New York: E. P. Dutton & Co., Inc., 1942), pp. 321-326.

[11] Adolph Harnack, *History of Dogma* (Boston: Roberts Brothers, 1895), vol. 1, p. 45.

[12] See Charles Norris Cochrane, *Christianity and Classical Culture* (New York: Oxford University Press, Inc., 1957).

[13] See Joseph Klausner, *From Jesus to Paul,* trans. William F. Stinespring (Boston: Beacon Press, 1943). This is the classic description of how a new major religion can appear.

[14] Reference is to Ernst Troeltsch's great distinction between "sect" type and "church" type in his *The Social Teaching of the Christian Churches*, 2 vols. (New York: Harper & Row, Publishers).

[15] This is the title of a volume in the life work of a great American Baptist, Kenneth Scott Latourette, *A History of the Expansion of Christianity*, vol. 7, (New York: Harper & Row, Publishers, 1945).

Chapter Six: Change and Revolution

[1] Tape of an address by Father Weigel.

[2] Adolf Harnack, *What Is Christianity?* (New York: G. P. Putnam's Sons, 1903), p. 224. Reprinted by permission of Ernest Benn Ltd., London.

[3] See Andrew Dickson White, *A History of the Warfare of Science with Theology* (New York: Appleton-Century-Crofts, 1897), vol. 1.

[4] Read William Barrett, *Irrational Man: A Study in Existential Philosophy* (New York: Doubleday & Company, Inc., 1958).

[5] See Alfred North Whitehead, *Science and the Modern World* (New York: The Macmillan Company, 1926).

[6] *Ibid.*

[7] See Karl Barth, "Creature," part 2 of *The Doctrine of Creation* which is vol. 3 of *Church Dogmatics* (Edinburgh: T. & T. Clark, 1960), pp. 3-19.

[8] See H. Richard Niebuhr, *Radical Monotheism & Western Culture* (New York: Harper & Row, Publishers, 1960) and *The Meaning of Revelation* (New York: The Macmillan Company, 1955).

[9] Alfred North Whitehead, *Adventures of Ideas* (New York: The Macmillan Company, 1933), particularly pp. 352-365.

[10] Shirley Jackson Case, *The Christian Philosophy of History* (Chicago: University of Chicago Press, 1943), p. 3.

[11] I.e., other than Catholic or Protestant as mere forms for faith, but the embodiment of Jesus' spirit and teaching in man.

[12] Harry Emerson Fosdick, *The Living of These Days* (New York: Harper & Row, Publishers, 1956), pp. 238-239.

[13] The three Furies (Alecto is implacable) is the symbol of unrelenting pressure toward one's end.

[14] See F. Van Der Meer, *Augustine the Bishop*, trans. Brian Battershaw (New York: Sheed and Ward, Ltd., 1961).

[15] In Jerusalem, working for decades on a Latin Bible, Jerome was bereft at the barbarian incursions against Rome.

[16] An ecumenical center of study and work at Lambuth Inn, Lake Junaluska, North Carolina, founded by Dr. Marney in 1967.

[17] See William Temple, *Nature, Man and God* (London: Macmillan & Co. Ltd., 1964).

[18] Pierre Teilhard de Chardin, *Hymn of the Universe* (New York: Harper & Row, Publishers, 1961), pp. 19f.

[19] *Ibid.,* pp. 19-37.

[20] Pierre Teilhard de Chardin, *The Phenomenon of Man* (New York: Harper & Row, Publishers, 1959), p. 213.

[21] Abraham Maslow, *Toward a Psychology of Being* (New York: Van Nostrand Reinhold Company, 1962). Also see Paul L. Lehmann, *Ethics in a Christian Context* (New York: Harper & Row, Publishers, 1963).

[22] Teilhard de Chardin, *The Phenomenon of Man,* p. 217.

[23] *Ibid.,* pp. 217-218.

[24] Adolf Harnack, *What Is Christianity?,* p. 130.

[25] *Ibid.,* p. 131.

[26] See H. Richard Niebuhr, *The Meaning of Revelation* (New York: The Macmillan Company, 1955), p. 183.

[27] Frederick Denison Maurice, *Theological Essays* (London: Macmillan & Co., Ltd., 1891), pp. 1-15.

[28] See Reuel L. Howe, *The Miracle of Dialogue* (New York: The Seabury Press, Inc., 1963), pp. 18-35.

[29] See Reinhold Niebuhr, *Faith and History* (New York: Charles Scribner's Sons, 1949), pp. 46f., 233, 30, 45, 103f.

[30] This is the title of a famous medieval work by Nicholas of Cusa. We are all "teachers of ignorance."

[31] The phrase is that of John Oman.

[32] Jacobus Arminius, one of Wesley's sources, emphasized faith as obedient work. Our own Reformed sources made much of faith as free gift.

[33] Title of Emil Brunner's great volume on the nature of man, *Man in Revolt* (Philadelphia: The Westminster Press, 1947).

[34] His concept of "progressive revelation" is really a notion of evolutionary development.

[35] A Statement of Faith designed to counteract Mullins' emphasis on psychological and ideological development in religion.

[36] A particularly vicious brand of localism which denies all other forms and frames of gospel except those of local congregations of believers immersed, etc. It is especially destructive to any real comprehension of "church."

[37] The repudiation in France of a Protestant sect that scattered thousands of middle-class French artisans over the world.

[38] Reference is to nineteen former board chairmen, at a church which I served, who took initiative on racial issues against the opposition of younger leaders.

45.83

121 / 550
48
70
60
100
90